engage

We've made it. Over 5   s,
we've looked at every
considered many different topics and hopefully read
loads together. If you've read all 20 issues — congratulations!
If not, you can still grab the rest. But for now, enjoy digging
into God's great word with Engage 20.

✳ DAILY READINGS Each day's page throws you into the Bible, to get you handling, questioning and exploring God's message to you — encouraging you to act on it and talk to God more in prayer.

THIS ISSUE: Peter encourages us to think straight and stand firm; **2 Chronicles** leads us back to God; **Mark** takes us to the cross; and **Proverbs** slaps us in the face. Hard.

✳ TAKE IT FURTHER If you're hungry for more at the end of an **engage** page, turn to the **Take it further** section to dig deeper.

✳ STUFF Articles on stuff relevant to the lives of young Christians. This issue: **pornography.**

✳ TRICKY tackles those mind-bendingly tricky questions that confuse us all, as well as questions our friends bombard us with. This time we ask: **Isn't Christianity just following a set of rules?**

✳ REAL LIVES True stories, revealing God at work in people's lives. This time we meet **Corrie ten Boom**, a real war heroine.

✳ ESSENTIAL Articles on the basics we really need to know about God, the Bible and Christianity. This issue, we ask: **What happens to people who reject Jesus?**

✳ TOOLBOX is full of tools to help you understand the Bible. This issue we discover how great it is to **read the Bible together.**

All of us who work on engage are passionate to see the Bible at work in people's lives. Do you want God's word to have an impact on your life? Then open your Bible, and start on the first engage study right now...

HOW TO USE engage

1 Set a time you can read the Bible every day

2 Find a place where you can be quiet and think

3 Grab your Bible, pen and a notebook

4 Ask God to help you understand what you read

5 Read the day's verses with engage, taking time to think about it

6 Pray about what you've read

BIBLE STUFF
We use the NIV Bible version, so you might find it's the best one to use with engage. If the notes say **"Read 1 Peter 1 v 2"**, look up 1 Peter in the contents page at the front of your Bible. It'll tell you which page 1 Peter starts on. Find chapter 1 of 1 Peter, and then verse 1 of chapter 1 (the verse numbers are the tiny ones). Then start reading. Simple.

In this issue...

ENGAGE 20 IS BROUGHT TO YOU BY:

Writers: Martin Cole   Cassie Martin   Helen Thorne
Design: Steve Devane   Andre Parker
Proof-readers: Anne Woodcock   Nicole Carter
Editor: Martin Cole (martin@thegoodbook.co.uk)

1 Peter

Pain before gain

Strangers and aliens in a hostile world, they face trial after trial, yet are shielded by an awesome power. Entrusted with a mystery from before all time, they must stand firm as they wait for the return of the king. No, it's not the latest fantasy epic from Hollywood, but the reality for the first readers of 1 Peter. And for Christians today too!

1 Peter is a letter written by the apostle Peter — you remember him; ex-fisherman, often spoke before he engaged his brain, let Jesus down badly but was forgiven and restored by Him. Peter wrote this letter to a group of Christians scattered all around the Mediterranean and Middle East.

These Christians were (a bit like their leader) chosen by God but rejected by men. They faced persecution. They struggled to be holy, just as we do. But like all who know Jesus, they had a great and inexpressible joy because they knew that they were forgiven and loved by God and that they had a wonderful future awaiting them.

Peter's letter reminds these Christians that living a life trusting Jesus will bring suffering before glory. Pain before gain. He tells believers that they don't belong on this earth — they have a new home to look forward to. And God's made sure they won't miss out when Jesus returns.

As you read 1 Peter, be encouraged to stand firm, thankful for what you have been saved from and excited about what you have been saved for!

1 | Perfect strangers

Ever been somewhere you've felt completely out of place in? A total stranger? Well, Peter says Christians are strangers, or exiles, in this world.

◉ Read 1 Peter 1 v 1–2

ENGAGE YOUR BRAIN

▶ *Who is writing the letter and how does he describe himself?*

▶ *What does that mean?*

▶ *Who is he writing to and where are they located?*

These Christians ("God's elect", God's chosen people) were scattered all over the area — probably after persecution. The authorities were trying to crack down on this new religion but the effect was like blowing on a dandelion — the seeds went everywhere and the gospel spread far and wide!

▶ *How do you think being "scattered" must have felt?*

▶ *How does Peter describe the life of a Christian? (v2)*

In the Old Testament, animal blood could be sprinkled on people to make them clean (or "sanctified") before God. This picture points us to Jesus, whose death can make people clean in God's sight. Notice that every member of the Trinity is intimately involved in calling someone to belong to God — Father, Son and Spirit (v2).

▶ *How does Peter greet these Christians? (end of v2)*

PRAY ABOUT IT

If we are members of God's family, grace and peace really are ours. Spend some time giving thanks to God for that now.

THE BOTTOM LINE

Christians are strangers in the world... but they are God's chosen people!

→ TAKE IT FURTHER

Find a little bit more on page 109.

2 | A new hope

Peter has hinted at the grace that these (and all) Christians have experienced, but the full reality is eye-poppingly good! Check out what it means to belong to Jesus!

👁 Read 1 Peter 1 v 3–7

ENGAGE YOUR BRAIN

▶ What has God done for us? (v3–5)

▶ What does that mean?

▶ What should be our response? (v3, 6)

▶ Why can we even rejoice in trials and tough times? (v6–7)

We don't tend to see much gold refining going on these days, but when mobile phones are recycled, they are put through something very similar so that the high temperatures melt away the rubbish and only the valuable metals needed to make new parts remain.

TALK IT OVER

Chat with another Christian about verses 6–7. Does it make it easier to know that hard times are being used by God to make you better and to bring praise to Jesus? How can you pray that this would be a comfort to you both?

👁 Read verses 8–12

▶ What deep joy does the Christian have? (v8)

▶ What does this emotion assure us of? (v9)

Jesus is nowhere to be seen, but Christians believe in Him, love Him, and are filled with joy as they think about the salvation (rescue) that God has achieved for them. Exciting!

PRAY ABOUT IT

Spend some time praising Jesus for who He is and all He has done for you.

THE BOTTOM LINE

Christians have a new birth and a living hope.

➔ TAKE IT FURTHER

Verses 10–12 explained on page 109.

3 | Look around you

A word to cyclists: looking down may help you avoid stones but OW! not parked cars. A word to Christians: for the full view, look up and ahead as well as back. That's what Peter says.

Read 1 Peter 1 v 13–16

ENGAGE YOUR BRAIN

- How does Peter begin verse 13?

It's a bit cheesy, but when you see a "therefore" in the Bible, you need to ask what it's there for!

- What has Peter been reminding his readers of in v1–12?
  - •
  - •
  - •
  - •
- How should Christians be in the present? (v13)
- What are they to look forward to in the future?

Bearing in mind all the amazing things God has done for us, we should be fired up to live for Him in the present. And if that wasn't enough, Peter reminds us that a glorious future awaits! So prepare your minds for action!

- How did Christians live before they were saved by Jesus? (v14)
- How can we and should we live now? (v15)
- What is our motivation? (v16)

GET ON WITH IT

A very wise Christian once said: "Be what you are". In Christ we are holy and blameless; we need to start living up to our new identity in Christ. BUT we can only do that in Him — with the help of His Holy Spirit, not just by making a bit more effort...

PRAY ABOUT IT

Ask God to help you remember His love and to have a mind that is alert and prepared for action. Thank Him that because Jesus is holy, we can be too. And pray for His Holy Spirit to enable you to live for Him.

→ TAKE IT FURTHER

Look forward to more on page 109.

4 Strange but true

Remember how Peter described his readers back in verse 1? More on what it means to be strangers in this world...

Read 1 Peter 1 v 17–22

ENGAGE YOUR BRAIN

▷ *Who are we trying to please? (v17)*

▷ *How much did it cost God to bring us into His family? (v18–19)*

▷ *How long has God had His rescue plan for? (v20)*

▷ *What has Jesus accomplished for us? (v21)*

▷ *Jesus has brought us into a new family — so how should we now live? (v22)*

GET ON WITH IT

Do you love other Christians? Even the weird or annoying ones? Ask God to change your heart so you start genuinely caring about them today! Talk to or sit with someone at church/youth group/CU because it will encourage them rather than make you feel comfortable.

Read verses 23–25

▷ *What is it that makes us able to live for ever? (v23–25)*

▷ *What would our natural state be? (v24)*

PRAY ABOUT IT

All people are like grass. We look good for a while but soon wither and die. It's only God's word — the good news about Jesus — that will make us live for ever. Pray for someone you know who is living like grass, that God would give them new birth into a living hope that lasts for ever.

THE BOTTOM LINE

The word of the Lord stands for ever.

→ TAKE IT FURTHER

More strangeness on page 110.

5 | Milking it

There's another "therefore" at the start of verse 1.
So what's it there for?

👁 Read 1 Peter 2 v 1–3

Remind yourself of some of the great things Peter has been talking about in the second half of chapter one. In particular, what is the word of God like and what does it do?

ENGAGE YOUR BRAIN

▶ *Bearing all that in mind, how does Peter urge these Christians to live? (v1–2)*

▶ *What are the negative things to stop doing? (v1)*

▶ *Can you put that in everyday language?*

▶ *What positive things should they do instead? (v2)*

▶ *What does that mean?*

THINK IT OVER

How would you describe your attitude to Bible reading? Remember that God's word saves you and gives you eternal life (1 v 23–25).

Do you crave it like a newborn baby desperate for milk? If not, why not?

▶ *What is the end goal of feeding on God's word? (end of v2)*

▶ *What do you think that means?*

▶ *What does Peter remind us of in v3?*

PRAY ABOUT IT

Ask God to give you an appetite for His word. Somebody once said that unlike eating normal food, the more we "eat" of the Bible, the hungrier we get! We want more and more!

THE BOTTOM LINE

Crave pure spiritual milk.

➔ TAKE IT FURTHER

More milk on page 110.

6 Love/hate relationship

There are some things that people either love or hate — in the UK it's a spread called Marmite! Sadly, in every country and throughout history, it's been Jesus. Read on to see why.

👁 Read 1 Peter 2 v 4–8

ENGAGE YOUR BRAIN

- ▶ *What is Jesus called in v4?*
- ▶ *What are the two ways He is described in the rest of v4?*
- ▶ *What are Christians called in v5?*
- ▶ *Why? (v5)*
- ▶ *How does the Old Testament describe Jesus? (v6)*
- ▶ *How has this come true for us? (v7)*
- ▶ *What else did the Old Testament predict? (v7–8)*
- ▶ *How has that come true?*

The cornerstone is the most important stone in a building — absolutely vital. Jesus is either essential and precious, or rejected and dangerous. You can't sit on the fence with Jesus — you're either for Him or against Him. We will stand or fall on how we respond to Him.

- ▶ *Have you thanked Him for dying in your place and acknowledged Him as Lord of your life?*

PRAY ABOUT IT

Pray for people you know who are currently rejecting Jesus, that they would see how precious He is and not stumble.

👁 Read verses 9–12

List the ways Peter describes Christians in v9–10.

-
-
-
-
-

Take some time to let these things sink in. Thank God for them. There's more explanation in *Take it further*.

- ▶ *So what does all this mean for us? (v11–12)*

THE BOTTOM LINE

You are a part of a chosen people.

→ TAKE IT FURTHER

Love it or hate it, there's more on page 110.

7 God's the boss

Christians don't belong in this world any more. We're strangers here, waiting for our new home with God. So, let's give up school, college, work. Ignore authority, drop out, enjoy our freedom, right? Not quite...

Read 1 Peter 2 v 13–17

ENGAGE YOUR BRAIN

▶ *What should Christians do? (v13–14)*

▶ *For what reason? (v13)*

▶ *Why does God want us to behave in this way? (v15)*

TALK IT OVER

Do you think it's always right to submit to our governments and authorities (police, teachers, parents etc)? Are there any exceptions? Chat with a Christian friend about this.

ENGAGE YOUR BRAIN

▶ *How does Peter describe us? (v16)*

Whether you were a slave back in Peter's day or have the most tyrannical boss (or parents!) today, Christians are truly free. We are free from sin and its consequences, thanks to the death and resurrection of Jesus. BUT, notice that Peter says

we shouldn't use our freedom to "get away with" anything now. Our lives should show we serve God rather than ourselves.

PRAY ABOUT IT

We can't do this on our own! It's hard to show respect for unfair teachers, corrupt politicians and our parents sometimes. But Jesus did it. Ask for the help of His Holy Spirit today.

▶ *How does Peter sum up this section? What are our duties to each of the people listed? (v17)*

GET ON WITH IT

How can you love other Christians, show honour to those in authority and, most importantly, fear (respect and serve) God today?

→ TAKE IT FURTHER

Serving suggestions on page 110.

8 | Suffering servant

However tough you have it, you're probably not living the life of a first-century slave...

ENGAGE YOUR BRAIN

▶ What is the surprise in v18?

▶ Why is it good to submit to and respect even harsh masters? (v19–21)

God is pleased with the heart attitude that seeks to do good even while being treated badly. But more than that, it's God's own attitude (v21).

▶ Whose example are we to follow? (v21)

▶ What did He do that we can follow? (v23)

▶ What did He do that He alone could do? (v24)

▶ Why should we follow Jesus?

PRAY ABOUT IT

Thank God for the wonderful news of verse 24. Thank Him for the comfort and reassurance of verse 25. Ask for the strength to be able to do good even when you're treated badly, remembering what Jesus did for you.

GET ON WITH IT

Learn 1 Peter 2 v 24 off by heart — you might be able to use it to explain to someone what Jesus has done.

THE BOTTOM LINE

Christ suffered for you.

→ TAKE IT FURTHER

A little more can be found on page 111.

STUFF

Porn

Porn seems to be everywhere. It's all over the internet, in books and even easy to reach on the shelves of shops. The temptation is there, within grasp. But what's so bad about looking at porn? Is it really such a big deal?

LUST

Lust is "strong sexual desire for someone or something that is not yours to have". It's not wrong to notice that someone is physically attractive — the problem is when that attraction gets out of control and leads to wrong sexual desires.

Pornography teases and tempts us to lust for something we shouldn't. This may be hardcore images or videos or it may be more subtle — "sexy" pics or passages about sex in books. Different things tempt different people. But if the outcome is lust and wrong sexual desires, then we should steer clear of it. 1 John 2 v 16 makes it clear that lust is from the world — not from God — so we should kick it out of our lives.

OBJECTS OF DESIRE

Porn can warp our view of other people. It makes us see the opposite sex as a group of body parts or the way to sexual fulfilment rather than a real person to have a real relationship with. We end up evaluating people by how physically attractive they are, rather than seeing them as someone made in the image of God.

Porn can mess with a man's view of masculinity. Instead of being a provider for and protector of women in his life, he learns that being a man means taking what you want from women with little care for them and no responsibility towards them.

Porn can also warp a woman's view of herself and her femininity. If a man's expectations are for a certain "look" or more flesh on show, then women often try to meet those expectations by how they look and dress. They can also devalue their opinion of themselves as if it's OK to be an object of lust or used for a quick fling.

REAL SEX

Real sex is very different to that depicted in pornography. Time, intimacy and a sense of being valued are needed to experience sexual fulfilment — not the few minutes of intense action of a porn scene. The expectation that in marriage, sex will be like it is in porn is totally unrealistic. It could taint your sex life, put emotional barriers up between you and your spouse and ruin the very thing you're after: good sex.

SEX ALONE

Surprisingly, the Bible doesn't specifically talk about masturbation. But, as we've seen, it does condemn lust. So when masturbation involves lustful thoughts of another person (and it usually does), it's definitely wrong. Masturbation is clearly not God's plan for sex. God designed sex to be between a man and a woman within marriage. The Bible is silent on masturbation so we have to be careful not to make sweeping statements about it. But it's very hard to masturbate without having lust-filled thoughts, so beware.

TAKING ACTION

So, how do we kick lust and porn out of our lives? Real lasting change must start from the inside with the knowledge that God has made you, Jesus loves you and the Holy Spirit wants to work in you, helping you to change. Don't think you're too disgusting for God. Say sorry to Him. If you're a Christian, Jesus has rescued you from sin and washed you clean. You're forgiven!

Take decisive action. Get rid of any magazines, DVDs, books or music that cause you to lust. Delete all pics, vids and bookmarks hidden on your computer or phone. Make sure there are locks on your internet use to stop you accessing porn. Use an Internet accountability programme. You'll be asked to name a number of people who will receive regular emails telling them what sites you have accessed. Try typing "accountability software" into your search engine and see what is available.

Move any computers or TVs out of your bedroom and into busier areas of your house. If being alone leads to temptation, make sure you're not home alone so often. Find a friend you trust and tell them about your problems with porn so they can check on how you're doing. Some of these things may seem extreme but we must take serious, immediate steps to kick sin out of our lives. Doing it gradually doesn't work.

God can help you deal with any sin problems. Jesus has already defeated sin. Talk to Him about it and with His help, kick it out.

Good books on this topic are: "Captured by a Better Vision", "Minizine: Purity in the age of Porn", and "Little Black Book: Sex". All available at thegoodbook.co.uk

2 Chronicles

It's a king thing

2 Chronicles is a book full of kings. There's a wise and wealthy one, one who was a mix of good and evil, and loads who turned away from God completely. There's one who murdered his brothers, one who listened to his evil mother, and one who threw his enemies off a cliff. And many more besides.

Some of Israel's kings trusted God, some were bad, some awful. But all serve to remind us that the way back to God's blessing is to walk His way, being devoted to Him.

But these kings are also pointers. In 2 Chronicles, Solomon is shown as the ideal king over God's people (chapters 1–9). But something's still wrong. God's people don't want God ruling over them, through Solomon.

And the pile of mostly bad kings (chapters 10–36) who follow Solomon points us ahead. We long for a perfect king over God's people who'll sort things out once and for all. And

so 2 Chronicles sends us scurrying into the New Testament... to Jesus.

1 & 2 Chronicles (it's one book, really) were written for God's people at a time (4th century BC) when they were a struggling minority, feeling insignificant and rejected. Maybe a bit like Christians feel nowadays.

Chronicles is designed to help God's people rediscover God and find a way back to all He's promised His people. The way back is to continue to walk His way.

9 | Wisdom or wealth?

David had been a great king, leading Israel in God's way. After David died, his son, Solomon, took on the role of God's chosen king. But what sort of a king would he be?

Read 2 Chronicles 1 v 1–6

ENGAGE YOUR BRAIN

▶ What's the great news about Solomon? (v1)

▶ And the reason for it? (v1)

▶ What did Solomon do? (v3, 6)

Like David (and unlike Saul), Solomon looked to God, wanting to serve Him. And recognising God's holiness, he set about ensuring that his sin and the sin of his people could be forgiven by God (v6).

Read verses 7–17

▶ How would you have responded to God's amazing offer? (v7)

▶ What did Solomon ask for? (v9–10)

▶ What did God think of Solomon's response? (v11–12)

▶ How did v12 come true? (v14–17)

King Sol recognised that God is in charge, is incredibly generous, all-knowing and sticks to His promises.

▶ Which of these aspects of God's character do you forget?

Solomon wasn't selfish, asking for riches or military strength — he just wanted to serve God and lead God's people wisely. This pleased the Lord and He promised to give Sol wealth and honour too.

As Solomon walked God's way — grasping God's promises and obeying Him — so he enjoyed God's blessing. The way to enjoy all the benefits and blessings Jesus brings us is to devote yourself to living His way.

PRAY ABOUT IT

Will you ask God to help you do that?

→ TAKE IT FURTHER

Grab some more on page 111.

10 | Hiram's helping hand

Sol's big task, first announced by God to David, was to build a house (temple) for God. Next, it's all temple-planning, wood-chopping, stone-cutting etc.

👁 Read 2 Chronicles 2 v 1–10

ENGAGE YOUR BRAIN

▶ What did Solomon say the temple was for? (v4)

▶ Why did it need to be great? (v5)

▶ What did Sol recognise about himself? (v6)

▶ What showed it would be a big task? (v2)

▶ What did Sol ask of the King of Tyre? (v7–8)

Would God live in the temple? In a way, yes: the temple was where He'd share His presence with His people. But no: there was no way any building could contain almighty God.

👁 Read verses 11–18

▶ What did Hiram recognise about God? (v12)

▶ And about Solomon? (v11–12)

▶ What would Hiram do for Sol? (v13–14, 16)

▶ What would he and his servants get in return? (v15)

Even the heathen king of Tyre recognised that God was behind Solomon. When any servant of God finds responsibility laid on them and takes it up as Sol did, God will support them and give them the ability to serve Him. And unbelievers will start to notice God at work.

PRAY ABOUT IT

Ask God to use you to serve Him. Pray that people around you will notice the great God who loves you.

THE BOTTOM LINE

God is great!

→ TAKE IT FURTHER

Help yourself to some more on page 111.

11 Behind the curtain

God had told David that his son Solomon would get to build a great temple for the Lord. At last, it's time for action.

👁 **Read 2 Chronicles 3 v 1–17**

ENGAGE YOUR BRAIN

▶ *Where did Sol build God's temple? (v1)*

▶ *What was significant about this place?*

▶ *What was the building like? (v4–7)*

▶ *What special area was built inside the temple? (v8)*

▶ *What closed off this place from the rest of the temple? (v14)*

This was thorough work with great attention to detail. It was expensive and impressive. Great splendour and richness.

▶ *What would the temple highlight about God?*

The Most Holy Place or "Holy of Holies" was the place where God was present. Ordinary people couldn't go behind the huge curtain into God's presence. Only the high priest was allowed in there, once a year.

👁 **Read Matthew 27 v 45–51**

▶ *As Jesus died, what happened? (v51)*

▶ *What does this show is the great achievement of Jesus' death?*

PRAY ABOUT IT

Thank Jesus that He died for your sin and removed the barrier so you can live with God. Ask Him to give you certainty that you're headed for perfect eternity in God's presence.

➡ **TAKE IT FURTHER**

Finishing touches on page 111.

12 Cloud control

Finally, the temple was completed. Time to bring the ark in, have a celebration and, who knows, maybe God Himself will make an appearance.

👁 Read 2 Chronicles 5 v 1–10

ENGAGE YOUR BRAIN

▶ *What was the first thing Sol did once the temple was built? (v1)*

▶ *Then what? (v2–3)*

▶ *What did they do when the ark arrived? (v6)*

▶ *Any idea why?*

▶ *What was in the ark? (v10)*

This was a significant moment for Israel. A house had been built for God. And now the ark — reminding them of God's covenant agreement with them — had arrived. This also reminded them of their role as God's chosen, obedient people; and of His promise to be with them.

👁 Read 5 v 11 – 6 v 11

▶ *What did the priests and Levites do? (5 v 11–13)*

▶ *Then what happened? (v13–14)*

▶ *What had God promised? (v4–9)*

▶ *How did it all come true? (v10–11)*

God kept His promises: He let Sol build Him a temple where He was now present among His people. What a great moment for the Israelites.

▶ *What did they recognise about God? (5 v 13)*

The Lord always keeps His promises. He's always with His people (Christians) and His love lasts for ever. And God expects them to love Him and live for Him.

PRAY ABOUT IT

What will you thank God for today?

THE BOTTOM LINE

God is good; His love lasts for ever.

→ TAKE IT FURTHER

Follow the cloud to page 111.

13 ¦ Sol speaks to God

The temple's complete; the ark's inside;
God is present there with His people.
King Solomon is excited and has loads
to say to God in front of everyone.

👁 Read 2 Chronicles 6 v 12–21

ENGAGE YOUR BRAIN

▶ What did Sol praise God for?
(v14–15)

▶ What did he ask from God?
(v16–17)

▶ What else? (v19–21)

Solomon could barely believe that
huge, all-powerful God would live
among His people. But knowing how
great and loving God is led Sol to ask
God to remember His people and
forgive them...

👁 Read verses 22–42

▶ What does Sol pray about?
v22–23:

v24–25:

v26–27:

v28–31:

v32–33:
v34–39:

v40–42:

▶ What does Solomon want to
happen? (v30, 33)

The king anticipated that God's
people would fail God and suffer for
it. But Solomon pleaded with God to
keep on forgiving His people as they
turned back to Him.

PRAY ABOUT IT
Follow Solomon's prayer pattern:
1. Praise God for what He's like.
2. Confess your sins to Him.
3. Ask for God's forgiveness.
4. Pray about what's on your mind.
5. Praise and thank Him some more.

→ TAKE IT FURTHER
Get to the heart of the matter on
page 112.

14 Words of warning

Life is looking great for God's people. Wise King Solomon is in charge, they have a shiny new temple in Jerusalem, and God is with them. What could possibly go wrong?

Read 2 Chronicles 7 v 1–10

ENGAGE YOUR BRAIN

▶ What had Solomon been praying about? (See yesterday's Engage and 6 v 22–42.)

▶ How did God respond? (7 v 1)

▶ What do you think this meant?

▶ What did the people think of it? (v3)

▶ Then what did they do? (v4–10)

God sending fire to burn up the people's sacrifices showed He accepted their offerings and accepted His people in His presence. Brilliant.

Read verses 11–22

▶ What was God's great news for Sol? (v12)

▶ What was His answer to Sol's earlier prayer? (v13–15)

▶ What else did He promise? (v16)

▶ What did God expect from Solomon? (v17–18)

▶ What was the warning? (v19–22)

Everything was going well for God's king and God's people. But it's often when life's going well that the devil attacks and we mess up big time. Solomon needed to listen to God's warning. And so do we. Sometimes we can cruise through life enjoying it so much that we fail to notice we're no longer obeying God. Or He's slipped way down our priorities.

PRAY ABOUT IT

Ask God, through His Holy Spirit, to help you be obedient to Him. Pray that when God warns you, you'll listen to Him.

→ TAKE IT FURTHER

Get some more on page 112.

15 God's king rules

Now it's time for the lowdown on King Solomon's reign. What did he actually do?

Read 2 Chronicles 8 v 1–11

ENGAGE YOUR BRAIN

▶ What did Solomon do during his time as king?
v1:
v2, 4–6:
v3:
v7–10:
v11:

God used Solomon to build a great kingdom. Solomon constructed a temple for God, a home for himself, one for his wife and loads for his people. He also built up his territory (v3) and his army so that Israel was protected. Under King Solomon, the Israelites lived in peace.

Read verses 12–18

▶ What did King Sol make sure happened regularly?
v12–13:
v14:

▶ What would Solomon be remembered for? (v16)

Solomon made sure God was worshipped properly during his time as king. Offerings were made to God, festivals were celebrated, priests and Levites were appointed, and the temple was completed. Solomon served God and wanted to ensure the people lived God's way and gave Him the praise He deserved.

THINK IT OVER

▶ Does your life reflect the fact that God's in charge?

▶ What do you do to ensure He gets the praise He deserves?

PRAY ABOUT IT

Ask God to give you a real desire to serve Him. Thank Him that because of Jesus, believers now have the Holy Spirit to help them live for God.

THE BOTTOM LINE

Believers live lives that worship God.

→ TAKE IT FURTHER

No *Take it further* today.

16 | Spice girl

God had given Solomon great wisdom and impressive wealth — and people started to hear about it. The queen of Sheba was curious to discover whether the rumours about Solomon and his God were true.

👁 Read 2 Chronicles 9 v 1–12

ENGAGE YOUR BRAIN

▶ What impressed this foreign queen? (v2–4)

▶ What did she realise about God? (v8)

The queen of Sheba was amazed by Solomon's wisdom and his impressive kingdom. And she saw where it came from — God had made Solomon king and given him all his wisdom and wealth. In return, God expected Sol to rule with justice and righteousness.

👁 Read verses 13–31

▶ What was Solomon given every year? (v13–14)

▶ What did he do with it? (v15–20)

▶ What else was Sol given? (v21)

▶ What amazing fact are we told about Solomon? (v22–23)

▶ Who was behind it all? (v23)

▶ Solomon was great but what happened to him in the end? (v31)

God had kept His promise to give Solomon wealth and wisdom. God's kingdom was in great shape. But it wouldn't last — the Israelites would turn away from God and life would never be as good again.

Yet one day there will be an even greater kingdom. Jesus will return to gather all believers to live in His perfect kingdom with Him. For ever.

PRAY ABOUT IT

Thank God for His gift of wisdom. Ask Him to give you a greater insight into what He's like and what He expects of you. And get ready for eternal life with the only perfect King — King Jesus.

→ TAKE IT FURTHER

Spice things up on page 112.

17 | Time to split

Solomon is dead, so Sol's son, Rehoboam, will take over as king of Israel. King of God's people. Will he walk God's way or will he and his kingdom crumble?

 Read 2 Chron 10 v 1 – 11 v 4

ENGAGE YOUR BRAIN

▶ What did the people want from their new king? (v4)

▶ What did the elders advise? (v7)

▶ But what did Rehoboam do? (v13–14)

▶ Why did all this happen? (v15)

After Solomon's death, rival Jeroboam led the Israelites to demand less forced labour, fewer taxes and less army service. Rehoboam took advice from the wrong people. Big mistake. Yet this was all part of God's plan (v15).

▶ What did most of Israel do? (v16, 19)

▶ Who stayed loyal to Rehoboam? (v17)

▶ What did Rehoboam plan next?

▶ What stopped him? (v4)

The Israelites told Rehoboam to take a hike and the kingdom split in two. Finally Rehoboam stopped making terrible decisions and listened to God. The Lord stepped in to stop him making even worse mistakes. God was still looking out for His people.

Skim read 11 v 5–23

▶ What did God's true people do? (v16–17)

▶ How does this challenge us?

God's kingdom was now split in two. Yet many people still had their hearts set on serving God and they supported Rehoboam in his new, smaller kingdom of Judah.

PRAY ABOUT IT

Ask God to help you listen to His warnings, seeking to live His way.

→ TAKE IT FURTHER

Let's split. Meet you on page 112.

18 | Ignoring God

God's people have split in two. Israel is the larger nation, but 2 Chronicles focuses on Judah because its kings are descended from God's chosen king, David. Let's see if Rehoboam walked in his grandfather's footsteps.

👁 Read 2 Chronicles 12 v 1–8

ENGAGE YOUR BRAIN

▶ What did the king and his people do when times were good? (v1)

▶ So what did God do? (v2–5)

▶ What did the king and his people do when times were hard? (v6)

▶ How did God respond? (v7)

▶ So what was the situation now for God's people in Judah? (v8)

▶ What would this teach them?

👁 Read verses 9–16

▶ What was the bad news? (v9)

▶ And the good news? (v12)

▶ What was special about Jerusalem? (v13)

▶ Yet how did God's special king treat the Lord? (v14)

▶ And what was the situation between God's people in Israel (ruled by Jeroboam) and Judah? (v15)

Jerusalem was God's city, where God was present among His people. But the people and their king ignored God. So the Lord let Egypt invade and carry away much of the wealth given to Solomon. As well as that, God's people were now two separate nations, at war with each other.

God wants His people to be humble (v12), realising how powerful and amazing He is — that He's their King. Ignoring God or turning away from Him will have serious consequences.

PRAY ABOUT IT

Pray for anyone you know who ignores God. Maybe that's you. Ask Him to transform their lives so they live with Him as their King.

➔ TAKE IT FURTHER

Don't ignore this; go to page 112.

19 Battle cry

Rehoboam's son, Abijah, became king of Judah.
But his nation was still at war with King Jeroboam
and Israel. Judah and Israel were both God's people
— would God take sides?

⊙ Read 2 Chronicles 13 v 1–9

ENGAGE YOUR BRAIN

▶ *Which army should win? (v3)*

▶ *Why did Abijah think God was on his side? (v5)*

▶ *Why did he think God was against Jeroboam?*
v6–7:
v8–9:

⊙ Read verses 10–12

▶ *What reasons did Abijah give for God being on Judah's side?*
v10:
v11:
v12:

Jeroboam had turned against God.
But many in Judah still worshipped
God. And their king was descended
from God's chosen king, David.
Maybe God would fight on their side.

⊙ Read 13 v 13 – 14 v 1

▶ *What happened? (v13–14)*

▶ *How did the smaller army win?*
v14:
v15:
v18:

▶ *What happened to Jerob'? (v20)*

▶ *And Abijah? (v21)*

The men of Judah were outnumbered
two to one and had been ambushed.
But they cried out to the Lord for
help and relied on Him to give them
victory. Weakness can be strength
when it causes us to rely on God
instead of ourselves.

GET ON WITH IT

▶ *In what areas do you need to rely on God more?*

▶ *What do you need to turn to Him for help with?*

▶ *Will you do that in prayer now?*

→ TAKE IT FURTHER

An alternative view on page 113.

25

20 Peace at last

David was a great leader of God's people. Solomon was mostly good. His son, Rehoboam, was mostly terrible. His boy, Abijah, was a good, God-serving king... for a while. But what about Abijah's son, Asa? Good king or bad king?

👁 Read 2 Chronicles 14 v 1–7

ENGAGE YOUR BRAIN

▶ What's the headline? (v1–2)

▶ What good stuff did Asa do?
v3, 5:
v4:
v6–7:

Awesome stuff. Asa wanted his people to obey God and he got rid of anything that might get in the way of this. God gave Judah peace and prosperity for 10 years. And then...

👁 Read verses 8–15

▶ What was the crisis? (v9)

▶ How did Asa react? (v11)

▶ What did he recognise about God?

▶ What did he do? (v12–14)

Asa and the people of Judah must have been feeling smug. Their land was peaceful, wealthy and well fortified. And then... a gigantic army appeared on the horizon, ready to crush them. But King Asa didn't panic; he turned to God for help. Asa trusted the Lord, knowing only God could give victory to their "powerless" army against such a mighty enemy. He was right, and God gave them an incredible victory. Nothing is impossible for God.

THINK IT OVER

▶ When do you feel powerless and useless as a Christian?

▶ Why are you not powerless?

▶ What do you need to ask God?

PRAY ABOUT IT

Thank God that He uses weak people like us in His plans. Ask Him to help you trust Him. Now tell Him what's on your mind.

→ TAKE IT FURTHER

More on Asa on page 113.

21 | Great start, terrible finish

King Asa trusted God and so Judah was at peace for many years. But would Asa stick with God his whole life?

👁 Read 2 Chronicles 15 v 1–19

ENGAGE YOUR BRAIN

▶ What's the good news and the bad news? (v2)

▶ What had happened in the past? (v3–6)

▶ So what was the message to King Asa? (v7)

▶ How did Asa respond? (v8)

▶ What about God's people?
v9:
v10–11:
v12:

▶ What was the result? (v15)

This was a step forward for God's people. They were taking God's word seriously, and so was their king. But...

👁 Read 2 Chronicles 16 v 1–14

▶ What new threat emerged? (v1)

▶ How did Asa react this time? (v2–3)

▶ What was the result? (v4–6)

▶ What were the more serious consequences? (v7–9)

▶ How did Asa respond to God's discipline? (v10, 12)

Asa trusted God for 36 years. And yet he stopped trusting the Lord and ended his reign with five bitter, angry years ignoring God's existence. Tragic. And so unnecessary.

THINK IT OVER

▶ What's the lesson for us here?

▶ What do you need to say to God today?

THINK IT OVER

Keep relying on God. Don't stop.

➔ TAKE IT FURTHER

A little more is on page 113.

Isn't Christianity just a set of rules?

Each issue in TRICKY, we tackle those mind-bendingly difficult questions that confuse us all, as well as questions that friends bombard us with to catch us off guard. This time we ask: Isn't Christianity mostly about following a set of rules?

Is Christianity just following a set of rules? Erm, the Ten Commandments? "Thou shalt not..." Case closed. But is that really what it's all about?

We tend to think that "playing by the rules" means you get ahead. And that's true for a lot of things. Brush your teeth regularly and you're unlikely to get many fillings. Do all your homework on time and your teachers will be pleased with you. But if you break the rules, you're out. Step over the line at bowling and it's a foul; your score won't count. Break the rules by smuggling a mobile phone into an exam and you'll forfeit your grade.

Is that what Christianity is like? Don't get drunk or have sex outside of marriage. Do turn up to church regularly and be a nice person. If we keep the rules, God will be pleased with us.

There are only two problems with that.
1) We can't keep the rules.
2) God is not interested in rule-keeping but in a relationship.

1. WE CAN'T KEEP THE RULES

The biggest rule-keepers in the Bible are probably the Pharisees. They usually get a bad press, but actually these guys were seen as super holy and mega respectable. But Jesus is far from impressed by them. Take a minute to read **Matthew 23**.

These rule-keepers were seen to be doing all the right things, making the right religious noises, but their hearts were miles from God (v28). In fact, Jesus calls them completely rotten (v27)! Interestingly, Jesus doesn't say that all the little rules are unimportant — He says that they should keep them as well as the big things like justice and mercy (v23).

It looks like if we really want to please God, we need to keep every single rule in the Bible and of course, we can't. We'll fall into the same trap as the Pharisees, if we think we can keep God happy by what we do. There is only one person who ever did that!

And a voice came from heaven: "You are my Son, whom I love; with you I am well pleased." (Mark 1v11)

By grace, we are given Jesus' perfect record and His perfect relationship with His Father because Jesus took the punishment for our sins at the cross. This leads us to the second point.

2. GOD DOESN'T WANT RULE-KEEPING; HE WANTS A RELATIONSHIP

God doesn't want us to just give Him the bare minimum — ten minutes Bible reading, the odd prayer and church attendance. That's not why Jesus died for us!

Revelation 5 v 9 talks about us being "purchased" by Christ's blood. He has bought us. He has redeemed us. He owns us. Marriage vows include the promise: "All that I am I give to you, all that I have I share with you". If we are Christians, we are the bride of Christ — we belong to Him. He gave Himself up for us and in loving gratitude we give ourselves to Him. We are saved by God's grace and we live by grace. It's a relationship built on love and dependence, not rule-keeping.

Good parents don't give up on their children when they break a rule or get things wrong. But break the law and you'll go to prison. Thankfully, God is not a giant policeman in the sky but our perfect Heavenly Father — He offers us forgiveness, love and the power to change.

Amazingly, Christianity is the only religion that offers us a perfect relationship with the living God. Far better than an impossible list of rules to keep!

29

22 | 1 Peter: Pain before gain

Today we return to Peter's first letter and a controversial subject — wives and husbands. As you read Peter's controversial words, remember that it's Jesus we are following.

👁 Read 1 Peter 3 v 1–2

ENGAGE YOUR BRAIN

▶ What does the "in the same way" refer back to? (Remind yourself of the end of chapter 2.)

▶ What is the possible result of this submission?

In the ancient world — and in some places today — you couldn't choose who you married. Some Christian women were in the difficult position of being married to a non-believer, or may have become Christians after their marriage. Either way (just like slaves with harsh masters) their Christ-like behaviour could win over their husband for Christ.

PRAY ABOUT IT

Pray for someone you know who is a Christian married to a non-Christian or who is the only Christian in their family. Ask God to help them be Christ-like in their behaviour so that they might draw attention to Jesus.

👁 Read verses 3–7

▶ What is the best way to be beautiful? (v3–4)

▶ How did Sarah honour God? (v6)

▶ Why might Christian wives be tempted to be afraid? (v6)

▶ What instructions does Peter give to Christian husbands? (v7)

▶ How would this have been against the culture of the time?

Men and women are both heirs of the gift of eternal life, so they're of equal worth in God's sight. BUT Peter says they need to show respect for one another in different ways. Both in Christ-like submission and in Christ-like care, consideration and respect.

THE BOTTOM LINE

Honour God by your behaviour.

→ TAKE IT FURTHER

More marriage guidance on p113.

23 Living in harmony

Our behaviour isn't just a way to communicate Christ to others; it's what God has called us to be like. Christianity isn't a hobby, it's a way of life.

👁 Read 1 Peter 3 v 8–9

GET ON WITH IT

▶ Who do you need to live more harmoniously with?

▶ Who will you be more sympathetic towards?

▶ Which Christians can you show brotherly/sisterly love to?

▶ When do you find it hard to be compassionate or humble?

▶ With the Holy Spirit's help, what do you need to do about that?

▶ Who do you like to insult or backstab?

▶ How will you be a blessing to them?

👁 Read verses 10–12

▶ What's the warning in these verses?

▶ What's the encouragement?

Peter is quoting Psalm 34. These verses were originally written to Old Testament believers — they are NOT saying that the way to get God to listen to you is to be good! The "righteous" in that psalm are not the morally good but those who "take refuge in the Lord" — people who turn to Him for help and mercy.

PRAY ABOUT IT

Ask for God's help to keep walking in His ways, to turn from evil and to do good. Pray about your answers to the earlier questions.

→ TAKE IT FURTHER

Turn harmoniously to page 113.

24 Stand up, speak out

It's often pretty scary being pointed out as a Christian, and as for telling (sometimes hostile) people why you are a Christian — eeek!

👁 Read 1 Peter 3 v 13–16

ENGAGE YOUR BRAIN

- ▷ *What might these Christians be worried about? (v13)*
- ▷ *What's the encouragement of v14?*
- ▷ *Why shouldn't Christians fear the same things as the world around us?*
- ▷ *What is it that changes our perspective? (v15)*

We might face mockery or social exclusion for being known as a Christian. Peter's first readers (and many Christians around the world) could face losing their income, physical attack or even death for following Christ. But we're not to fear these things; we're to fear God (2 v 17). And Peter reminds us that if we suffer for doing good, we're blessed by Him.

- ▷ *Instead of being frightened, what should we do? (v15)*
- ▷ *How should we do this? (v15–16)*
- ▷ *Hopefully, what will the outcome then be?*

TALK IT OVER

Chat with another Christian about how you can explain your beliefs in a gentle and respectful manner. Do you find it scary? Then pray together that you won't fear people, but God. Do you tend to get argumentative or pushy when trying to show how Christianity is the truth? Then pray together for a spirit of gentleness and respect. Remember that Christ is Lord and ask for the courage to show and tell that.

PRAY ABOUT IT

Pray that you would see Christ as He really is — Lord of everything — and that you wouldn't be scared to be known as His follower.

THE BOTTOM LINE

In your heart, set apart Christ as Lord.

→ TAKE IT FURTHER

Don't be afraid — turn to page 114.

25 | Christ's perfect example

Suffering and Jesus — two themes that Peter returns to again and again.

👁 Read 1 Peter 3 v 17–22

ENGAGE YOUR BRAIN

▶ What does Peter remind us of again in v17?

▶ Who does he point us to again and why? (v18)

▶ Why was Jesus' death far from pointless? (v18)

GET ON WITH IT

Learn 1 Peter 3 v 18 — it's a wonderful explanation of the amazing swap that took place at the cross.

Verses 19–22 have caused many people to scratch their heads over the years — what exactly is Peter referring to? We'll start with what is clear!

▶ According to v20, how did most people respond to God in the days of Noah, (and now!)?

▶ Who was saved and how?

▶ What truth does baptism remind us of? (v21)

▶ What is it that saves us? (v21–22)

▶ What are we reminded about Jesus? (v22)

See *Take it Further* for more on these tricky verses.

PRAY ABOUT IT

Ask God to help you pass the message of v18 on to those who are currently rejecting their Creator. Thank Him that if we trust in Jesus, we can be washed clean inside, just as baptism makes us clean outside.

THE BOTTOM LINE

Jesus died for your sins, to bring you to God.

→ TAKE IT FURTHER

Get your head around these tricky verses on page 114.

26 | Living for God

Suffering. It's not exactly appealing, is it? But, as Peter reminds us, it's the sign of a serious Christian.

👁 Read 1 Peter 4 v 1–7

ENGAGE YOUR BRAIN

▶ What's the "therefore" there for? What has chapter 3 been reminding us about?

▶ Which attitude of Christ's are we to imitate? (v1)

▶ What are we living for? (v2)

▶ If we are not living for God, what are we living for? (v2)

▶ What does this look like in practice? Try putting v3 into everyday language.

▶ What will be the outcome of not joining in? (v4)

Have you ever experienced this? Being mocked or excluded for going God's way can feel pretty miserable.

▶ How is v5 an encouragement to Christians who are persecuted for their changed behaviour?

GET ON WITH IT

We will all have to give an account to God for the life we've lived. The good news is that we can have Jesus' perfect record because He paid all our debts on the cross. Can you share this with someone today?

PRAY ABOUT IT

Read verse 7. How will remembering this help you to pray? What sort of things can you be praying about from the previous verses? Do it!

THE BOTTOM LINE

Live for Jesus; He died for you.

→ TAKE IT FURTHER

More lifestyle tips on page 114.

27 Love above all

Love one another; so simple yet so difficult. Jesus said it was the second most important commandment and a sign of being one of His followers.

👁 Read 1 Peter 4 v 8–11

ENGAGE YOUR BRAIN

▶ *Why is loving each other so important? (v8)*

▶ *What might this look like in practice? (v9–10)*

Ever grumble about having to hang out with people at church who are a bit weird? Or being made to welcome new people at youth group instead of chatting to your friends? Loving each other is often inconvenient, but it's what Jesus wants us to do. It also helps us to forgive people when they do us wrong (v8).

God gives all Christians different gifts.

▶ *What are these gifts for? (v10)*

▶ *What does Peter remind us that we are administering (sharing) or being stewards of?*

▶ *What should be the end result?*

(v11)
So whether you're good at music, make a mean cappuccino, can stack and put away 100 chairs in ten minutes or can lead a great Bible study, remember that it's not about you. You're here to serve others in God's strength so that He gets the glory. Got it?

PRAY ABOUT IT

Thank God for His grace to you — shared with you by other people who teach and serve you at church (Why not thank them too?). Ask for God's strength to serve others and to glorify Him.

THE BOTTOM LINE

Above all, love one another deeply.

→ TAKE IT FURTHER

More love stuff on page 114.

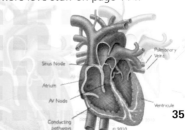

28 Painful reading

Peter keeps reminding us that the Christian life involves suffering. But is it really worth it?

Read 1 Peter 4 v 12–19

ENGAGE YOUR BRAIN

▶ *What might our reaction to suffering be? (v12)*

▶ *But how should we respond to suffering?*

▶ *What does Peter remind us? (v14)*

▶ *How might we be tempted to feel when suffering? (v16)*

▶ *What does Peter say we should do instead?*

THINK IT OVER

Can you think of examples in the media recently where someone has suffered for being a Christian? Can you think of any examples in your own life?

▶ *What does Peter call us in v17?*

▶ *How does that make you feel?*

▶ *If things are tough now for Christians how much tougher will they ultimately be for others? (v17–18)*

▶ *What is Peter's encouragement to his readers and us in v19?*

▶ *How does Peter describe God?*

PRAY ABOUT IT

God is faithful — we follow a suffering Saviour, and although we will face trouble, we are part of His family and more blessed than we can imagine. Spend some time now praising and thanking God that you belong to Him.

→ TAKE IT FURTHER

No pain, no gain. Page 115.

29 Relationship advice

More about our relationships with other Christians and our relationship with God, as Peter gets towards the end of his great letter.

👁 Read 1 Peter 5 v 1–4

ENGAGE YOUR BRAIN

▷ *Who does Peter address first of all? (v1–4)*

▷ *What word does he use to sum up the way they should lead God's people? (v2)*

▷ *What are the dos and don'ts in v2–3?*

▷ *Who is the Chief Shepherd? (v4)*

▷ *What should ultimately motivate Christian leaders? (v4)*

PRAY ABOUT IT

Pray for your church leaders / youth leaders, that they would have these characteristics and that they would receive the crown of glory when Jesus returns.

👁 Read verses 5–7

▷ *Who does Peter advise next? (v5)*

▷ *What does he tell them to do? (v5)*

Whether you're overseeing other people or submitting to another's lead, humility is the key. If you find yourself thinking you're more important than another Christian, you shouldn't be in leadership.

▷ *How does God react to the proud? (v5)*

▷ *Who determines our worth and status? (v6)*

▷ *So how should we respond to Him and why? (v6–7)*

PRAY ABOUT IT

Verse 7 — do it now.

THE BOTTOM LINE

Humble yourself, so that God may lift you up.

→ TAKE IT FURTHER

Another top tip on page 115.

30

In conclusion...

Closing words now — the things Peter really wants his original readers (and us) to hang onto.

👁 Read 1 Peter 5 v 8–11

▶ *What two things does Peter tell us to be in v8?*

▶ *Why do we need to be on our guard?*

▶ *What will encourage us to stand firm in the faith? (v9)*

▶ *How might the devil use suffering or persecution to tempt us away from our faith?*

▶ *Who is really in control? (v10)*

▶ *How will He help us? (v10)*

A wise Christian minister once said: "Suffering can make you bitter or it can make you better". Get your head round how God can use suffering and persecution for our good BEFORE it happens, so that you don't fall apart when it inevitably comes.

👁 Read verses 12–14

▶ *How does Peter sum up the message of his letter in v12?*

▶ *How does Peter describe Silas and Mark?*

Mark wasn't biologically related to Peter, but Peter treated him like a son. This is the guy who wrote Mark's Gospel, which appears to be largely based on Peter's testimony.

▶ *What is Peter's final blessing to those who are in Christ? (v14)*

PRAY ABOUT IT

Pain before gain. Suffering before glory. The Christian life will be tough. But God won't forget He's called you to share in His eternal glory. Think how 1 Peter's prepared you to keep going as a Christian. Thank God for this letter. And ask for His help not to give up.

→ TAKE IT FURTHER

Concluding remarks — page 115.

31 | Psalms: Bad times, good times

We're going to spend three days reading some of David's psalms — his songs and prayers to God. In this psalm, we see David's reaction to severe pressure. Life seems too much for him.

👁 Read Psalm 143 v 1–6

ENGAGE YOUR BRAIN

▶ *What does David ask for? (v1–2)*

▶ *What does David recognise about God? (v1)*

▶ *What's been happening? (v3)*

▶ *How has it affected David? (v4)*

▶ *Do you ever feel like that?*

David remembers how good God has been to him in the past — but it all seems so long ago (v5).

👁 Read verses 7–12

▶ *Which phrases show how urgent David's prayer is? (v7–8)*

▶ *Why is v8 a good example of prayer?*

▶ *What does it mean to hide yourself in God? (v9)*

▶ *How does such a person want to live? (v10)*

David is at a very low point. But he knows God is faithful and righteous and will hear his prayers. We're not told the outcome; we're just left with a reminder of God's unfailing love to His people (v12).

Dark times *do* come: times of trouble, doubt, opposition, struggle. When they do, remember this — you're not the first. You're not alone. You're not without help. A crisis is the opportunity to take hold of the faithful God. Will you do that?

PRAY ABOUT IT

What tough stuff do you need to pray about? Who do you know who's really low at the moment? Pray that they will cling to God, trusting in Him to lift them up.

→ TAKE IT FURTHER

Prayer tips — page 115.

32 Rock solid

David's in trouble again. This time his army is facing defeat at the hands of godless foreign invaders. So guess where King David turns for help.

👁 Read Psalm 144 v 1–4

ENGAGE YOUR BRAIN

▶ What truths about God does David sing? (v1–2)

▶ How do humans compare to God? (v3–4)

God is our "Rock" — He's strong, never changes, is trustworthy and we can turn to Him for refuge and safety. He looks after us. He is both a "loving God" and a strong "fortress" (v2). Compared to God, we're nothing. Yet He cares for us, protects us and answers our prayers!

👁 Read verses 5–15

▶ What does David ask God to do? (v5–8)

▶ What shows his confidence in God? (v9–10)

▶ What does he look forward to?
v12:
v13:
v14:

▶ How does David describe God's people? (v15)

In this psalm we see a king who is given victory by God and who benefits his people. Of course, we're pointed to the Lord Jesus Christ. Those who trust in Jesus share in the benefits of His victory and look ahead to a glorious, eternal future.

PRAY ABOUT IT

Go on. Shimmy round your room in celebration. And tell God your response to this psalm. Just how great is God?

THE BOTTOM LINE

God is our rock and fortress.

→ TAKE IT FURTHER

No Take it further today.

33 | The truth about God

Write down five things your non-Christian friends say about God (Eg: He doesn't exist, He's out of touch etc). With that in mind, let's jump into an explosively enthusiastic psalm.

👁 **Read Psalm 145 v 1–7**

ENGAGE YOUR BRAIN

▶ *What specific things is David excited about?*

▶ *Which strikes you most?*

👁 **Read verses 8–16**

▶ *How is God described here?*

▶ *How involved is He with His world? In what ways?*

THINK IT OVER

▶ *Can you think of examples from your own life of v8, 14 and 16?*

👁 **Read verses 17–21**

▶ *What encouragements are here?*

▶ *And what warnings?*

David's own words give us a clue as to what our response to God should be.

▶ *Is your response the same as v1–2 and v21?*

▶ *List all the ways David expects others to respond (v3–7).*

All those responses are about communication: talking to God and others about how great God is.

SHARE IT

Remember your friends' views?

▶ *How will you share the great news of God with them?*

▶ *Why is it so important we do that? (v20)*

PRAY ABOUT IT

The first step is to get praying: for your friends, for your knowledge of God and enthusiasm for Him. As you seek to live His way, pray for chances to talk about how great He is.

→ **TAKE IT FURTHER**

More truths on page 115.

41

REAL LIVES

Unlikely war hero

The ten Booms were a Christian family living in the town of Haarlem in Holland when the Nazis invaded and occupied their country in 1940. The family became involved with the Resistance movement, who opposed their German occupiers.

In May 1942, a woman came to the ten Boom door with a suitcase in her hand. She told them she was a Jew and, as Occupation authorities had recently visited her, she was afraid to return home. Having heard that the ten Booms had helped her Jewish neighbours, she asked if she might stay with the family. Corrie's father, Casper, readily agreed.

Youngest daughter Corrie and her sister Betsie began taking in refugees — both Jews and members of the Resistance — who were in hiding. There was room in the house but food was scarce for everyone due to wartime shortages. Every (non-Jewish) Dutch person received a ration card which was required to obtain weekly coupons to buy food.

Corrie remembered a disabled girl she'd looked after, whose father was in charge of the local ration-card office. She went to his house one evening, and he seemed to know why. When he asked how many ration cards she needed, "I opened my mouth to say, 'Five,'" Corrie wrote in The Hiding Place. "But the number that unexpectedly came out instead was: 'One hundred.'" He gave them to her, and she provided them to every Jew she met.

Because of the number of people using their house, the ten Booms built a secret room in case a raid took place. Gradually, family and supporters brought bricks and other building supplies into the house in briefcases and rolled-up newspapers. When finished, the secret room was less than a metre wide and only accessible through a built-in cupboard. It had a small air vent on an outside wall and inside, a mattress, biscuits and water. Up to six people would cram into this space when a special alarm was given.

The whole operation ended in February 1944 when someone tipped off the Gestapo, who immediately raided the house. Nazis found evidence of Resistance documents and arrested the family for possessing illegal ration-cards. However, they never did find the concealed room nor its last occupants. Corrie's father, Casper, sadly died after 10 days in German custody, and the sisters saw three prisons in ten months, ending up in the infamous Ravensbrück concentration camp, where they spread the Christian message among the female prisoners. In late 1944, Betsie succumbed to illness and died, a huge blow to Corrie, who had relied on her faith and inspiration. Before she died, Betsie told Corrie: "There is no pit so deep that God's love is not deeper still".

Corrie miraculously escaped death in the Ravensbrück gas chambers, thanks to an incredible clerical error, and returned to Holland. Once the

Allies had defeated the Germans, she began speaking in public about her story and her faith in Christ. She set up a home for war refugees and ex-prisoners of the Germans. She even offered shelter to German collaborators, as long as they agreed to give medical and psychological support to the other residents. Because her sin had been forgiven by Jesus, she was able to show forgiveness to, and work with, her former enemies.

After the war, Corrie visited more than 60 countries in 33 years, sharing her story and faith everywhere she went. In the 1970s, she moved to the U.S. where she wrote the bestseller *The Hiding Place*, which was also made into a movie. Corrie died in 1978 on her 91st birthday, having openly served Christ for many years.

In her book *Tramp for the Lord*, she tells the story of an encounter with a former Ravensbrück camp guard who had been known as one of the most cruel. She was reluctant to forgive him, but prayed that she would be able to. Corrie wrote: "For a long moment we grasped each other's hands, the former guard and the former prisoner. I had never known God's love so intensely as I did then." She also wrote that in her post-war experience with other victims of Nazi brutality, it was those who were able to forgive who were best able to rebuild their lives.

Mark

The end

This is the end. As we reach the end of Mark's Gospel, Mark talks us through the end of Jesus' life on earth; and Jesus talks about the end of Jerusalem and the end of the world.

So we need to read this section of Mark with our eyes wide open, taking in Jesus' warnings and vital teaching. But also looking to the perfect future that is guaranteed for those who trust in Him.

It all sounds a bit morbid, doesn't it? Well, yes there is some tough stuff in these closing chapters: the destruction of God's temple, false teachers, loads of warnings, and some downbeat predictions from Jesus. And then Jesus' arrest, betrayal (by one of His disciples), trial and death. Not the funniest of topics.

But...

There are glimpses of a glorious future too. Jesus hints at an amazing return for the "Son of Man". Jesus' death would not be the end. It would be the beginning of an incredible, eternal future for His followers.

34 | Birth pains

There are horrific wars and terrorist attacks all over the world. They shock and appal us when we hear about them. But nothing shocks Jesus. He knew all of these things would happen.

👁 Read Mark 13 v 1–8

ENGAGE YOUR BRAIN

▶ What impressed this disciple? (v1)

▶ What was Jesus' surprising reply?

▶ What did the disciples want to know? (v4)

▶ How might they be deceived into thinking the end was near? (v5–8)

▶ Did these events mean the end was near? (end of v8)

Jesus predicted that God's temple in Jerusalem would be destroyed (it was, 40 years later). The disciples wondered if this would be the start of the end of the world. Jesus said loads of scary stuff would happen. But these were just the beginning of "birth pains" — clues that the end was coming at some point.

👁 Read verses 9–13

▶ Who would be against Jesus' followers? (v9, 12–13)

▶ What must believers remember when they face opposition?
v10:
v11:
v13:

Christians must expect to be given a hard time. Many people hate the message of Jesus and will turn against us. But we have a responsibility to tell people about Jesus. The great news is that God has given us the Holy Spirit to help us to stand up for Jesus and even to put words into our mouths. Those who stand by Jesus to the end will live with Him for ever!

PRAY ABOUT IT

Ask God to give you the words to tell others about Him and to stand up to any hassle you get. Thank God for giving you His Holy Spirit to help you actually do it.

→ TAKE IT FURTHER

No pain, no gain — page 115.

35 Scary stuff

Jesus is telling His disciples that Jerusalem will be destroyed. He's also talking about the end of the world. Scary stuff!

Read Mark 13 v 14–20

ENGAGE YOUR BRAIN

▶ *Any idea what Jesus is talking about?*

▶ *What's the good news? (v20)*

Jesus is predicting the destruction of God's temple in Jerusalem. This happened when the Romans trashed Jerusalem in AD70. So what is v14 talking about exactly?

Well, Bible experts continue to argue about what the abomination / destroying terror / horrible thing is. What's clear is that Mark's talking about God's temple being mistreated and disrespected. This was predicted 600 years earlier by Daniel (it's in Daniel 9 v 25–27).

Terrible times are promised (v18–20). Worse than ever before. But because of God's amazing love for *the elect* (His chosen people, Christians), these times won't last for long.

Read verses 21–23

▶ *What does Jesus warn us to watch out for?*

If anyone claims to be Jesus or to be God's special messenger, don't believe them. They're out to deceive you. It sounds obvious, but even strong Christians can be fooled. When Jesus comes again, we'll all recognise Him!

PRAY ABOUT IT

Thank God that despite all the terrible things that happen in the world, He's in control. He looks after His people. And pray that you won't be fooled by false teachers.

→ TAKE IT FURTHER

Don't be scared; go to page 116.

36 Unmissable

On the news we sometimes see people telling us when they think the world will end. Some even climb up mountains or tall buildings so they'll be the first to see Jesus coming!

👁 Read Mark 13 v 24–27

ENGAGE YOUR BRAIN

▶ What will make Jesus' return unmissable? (v24, 25, 26)

▶ What's reassuring for God's people, "the elect"? (v27)

That's completely different from the way Jesus came into the world the first time — born as an unknown baby, sleeping in an animal trough. This time everyone will see that He is the King of kings. Everyone will know exactly who He is.

👁 Read verses 28–31

Jesus is talking about the temple again. There would be clues that its end was coming. They could be sure it would happen like this because everything Jesus says is true, hugely important and will last for ever (v31).

👁 Read verses 32–37

▶ Do we know when Jesus will come back? (v32–33)

▶ Why do we need to be ready? (v35–36)

GET ON WITH IT

▶ Are you ready for Jesus' return?

▶ Are you living for Him?

▶ Are you telling your friends about Jesus, that He can rescue them?

PRAY ABOUT IT

Thank Jesus that you can trust Him completely and that He will take Christians to live with Him for ever. And ask Him to help you serve Him while you're waiting for His return.

→ TAKE IT FURTHER

Don't miss *Take it further* on page 116.

47

37 : The plot thickens

It's nearly time for the huge Passover feast, so Jesus, His disciples and thousands of Jews are all heading to Jerusalem. On His way, Jesus stops off at the village of Bethany, just outside Jerusalem.

Read Mark 14 v 1–11

ENGAGE YOUR BRAIN

▶ What did the religious leaders have planned? (v1–2)

▶ What excited them? (v10–11)

▶ Where was Jesus? (v3)

Strange customs of the day:
1) Lying down to eat.
2) Dinner parties were normally men only.
3) Oil on the head showed respect. And if you don't know what nard is, join the club.

▶ Why were some of the other guests cheesed off? (v4–5)

▶ How did Jesus respond? (v6)

▶ Why did Jesus defend her?
v7:
v8:

This woman poured a whole jar of expensive perfume over Jesus' head. She was showing how much she loved Him. Some people thought it was a waste of perfume and money. But Jesus said it was a beautiful thing, which is why we're reading about it 2000 years later (v9).

The gospel focuses on Jesus' death, as this woman did. And she was extravagant in her worship of Jesus; no holding back.

GET ON WITH IT

▶ How can you make sure you focus more on Jesus' death?

▶ How do you hold back worship from Jesus?

▶ How can you be more extravagant in your worship?

PRAY ABOUT IT
Talk to God about these things.

→ TAKE IT FURTHER
There's some more on page 116.

38 | Meal deal

Jerusalem was crammed with thousands of people ready to celebrate Passover. Each family needed a room to cook and eat a Passover lamb together. Jesus wanted to eat His final Passover feast with His disciples.

But in this overcrowded city, where could they possibly find a room to eat together?

👁 Read Mark 14 v 12–16

▶ *What were Jesus' bizarre instructions?*

▶ *What happened? (v16)*

👁 Read verses 17–21

▶ *What shocking news did Jesus announce?*

▶ *How did the disciples respond?*

▶ *How do we know God was in control? (v21)*

▶ *Did this let Judas off the hook? (v21)*

Even before Jesus was born, the Old Testament said that God would send someone to rescue His people. That person was Jesus. But the Old Testament also said that He would have to suffer and die to rescue us

(Isaiah 53 v 5). Amazingly, it was all part of God's rescue plan!

Judas did a terrible thing. He would be punished for it later. But Judas couldn't stop God's perfect plans. Nobody can! Instead, Judas himself became part of God's great rescue plan! Incredible.

PRAY ABOUT IT
Thank God that no one stops His perfect plans to rescue people.

→ TAKE IT FURTHER
The origins of Passover — page 116.

39 | The bread of life

What's the most memorable meal you've eaten? What made it special? Today we read about the most important meal ever.

👁 Read Mark 14 22–26

ENGAGE YOUR BRAIN

▶ *What did Jesus do with the bread? (v22)*

▶ *How would you explain what He meant?*

Only a few hours before His death, Jesus used this meal to show His disciples what He was about to go through for them. The broken bread was a symbol of Jesus' body, which would be broken by torture and crucifixion. Eating the bread showed the disciples that they would share in the good that came from Jesus' death for them.

▶ *What was the significance of the wine? (v24)*

Blood gives life to our bodies. When Jesus died on the cross, He gave His life for others. Drinking the wine reminded the disciples that Jesus would give His life for them, so their sins could be forgiven.

Blood of the covenant (v24): a covenant is an agreement where God promises to forgive people for their sin. But only people who trust Jesus' death to rescue them from the punishment they deserve.

Christians still eat bread and drink wine together to remember that Jesus died for them. This meal is called the Lord's Supper or Communion.

THINK IT OVER

▶ *Take time to work out how you can explain (in your own words) why Jesus' death is good news.*

PRAY ABOUT IT

Got anything to thank God for today?

THE BOTTOM LINE

Jesus gave His life for you. Never forget it.

➡ TAKE IT FURTHER

Feast some more on page 117.

40

Stand and deliver

It's night time on the Mount of Olives and danger is approaching for Jesus. Will the disciples face it with Him or run away?

👁 Read Mark 14 v 27–31

ENGAGE YOUR BRAIN

▶ What did Jesus predict? (v27)

▶ What great promise seemed to go unnoticed? (v28)

▶ How did Peter react to it all?

▶ What big claim did he make?

▶ But what did Jesus know? (v30)

Jesus told His disciples that they'd all leave Him when trouble came. Just like sheep scattering when they're scared! Peter refused to believe it, but Jesus knew what would happen.

Standing up for Jesus can be really hard. We don't want people to give us a hard time for going to church or believing in Jesus. So we find it hard to own up to being a Christian. Or we keep quiet when people say things against Jesus.

Jesus had already told His followers that they should expect to get hassled for loving Him (it's in Mark 13 v 9-11). But He also told them that He'd help them out in tricky situations (Mark 13 v 11).

THINK IT OVER

▶ When have you deserted Jesus?

▶ When do you find it hard to stand up for Him?

▶ Do you want to change?

▶ How will this happen?

PRAY ABOUT IT

Ask God to help you stand up for Jesus. Ask Him to give you the right words to say, and the courage to say them.

→ TAKE IT FURTHER

What's Zechariah got to do with anything? Answers on page 117.

41 Garden of grief

The disciples don't seem to realise it, but Jesus is nearing His death. And He knows it. Bear this in mind as you read today's highly emotional section of Mark's Gospel.

👁 Read Mark 14 v 32–36

ENGAGE YOUR BRAIN

▷ Why do you think Jesus was so upset?

▷ What did He ask for? (v35–36)

▷ Yet what did He want most of all? (end of v36)

Jesus knew His Father was about to punish Him for the sins of the world. He didn't deserve to die, but it was the only way He could rescue us. No wonder Jesus fell to the ground in distress. No wonder He asked God to *"take this cup from me"*.

He was asking God not to punish Him. He knew it would be like drinking from a cup full of God's anger. Yet Jesus wanted to obey His Father God, even though that meant He would have to suffer and die!

👁 Read verses 37–42

▷ What did Jesus say to His disappointing disciples? (v38)

▷ What did Jesus know was about to happen? (v41–42)

Like these three disciples, all Christians need to **watch and pray**. The devil is always trying to tempt us to sin. So we need to **watch** out for anything that might cause us to disobey God. And we need to **pray**, asking God to help us obey Him.

THINK IT OVER

▷ What have you learned today?

▷ What has really challenged you?

▷ Anything you need to do?

PRAY ABOUT IT

Read today's verses again and then talk honestly with God.

➔ TAKE IT FURTHER

Good grief. Turn to page 117.

42 Arrested development

Jesus is in the garden of Gethsemane late at night. Suddenly, the silence is disturbed, as an angry crowd comes to capture Jesus...

👁 Read Mark 14 v 43–52

ENGAGE YOUR BRAIN

▶ What made Judas' betrayal so hideous? (v44–45)

▶ Why wasn't Jesus surprised? (Mark 14 v 18)

▶ Who was behind the arrest? (v43)

▶ How did one of the disciples fight back?

▶ What did Jesus say about His arrest? (v48–49)

▶ Then what happened? (v50–52)

▶ What had Jesus said in Mark 14 v 27?

What a disaster! At first sight, it looks as if everything's gone wrong. Judas has turned against Jesus; Jesus has been captured; and His friends have deserted Him. How could this be part of God's rescue plan?

But Jesus knew all this would happen; He'd predicted it. In fact, the Old Testament (Zechariah 13; Isaiah 53) had predicted it centuries earlier. The scene was disturbing and depressing but it was all part of God's great rescue plan. God was in control even in the darkest of moments.

THINK IT OVER
Read through this story again, verse by verse, thinking about how each bit makes you feel.

▶ What effect does it have on you and why?

THE BOTTOM LINE
Jesus suffered and died to rescue us from sin.

PRAY ABOUT IT
Spend time thanking God for His perfect plan to rescue us.

➔ TAKE IT FURTHER
Encouragement from Peter on p117.

53

ESSENTIAL

Eternal death

In *Essential*, we take time out to explore key truths about God, the Bible and Christianity. This issue, we look at hell and what happens to people who reject Jesus.

THE GOOD NEWS

Christianity is good news. It's great news! It's the message that through Jesus, sinful human beings can be forgiven, come back into relationship with their Creator and enjoy eternal life in a place of complete perfection. When Jesus returns, those who follow Him will be able to face the judgment He brings with absolute confidence — safe in the knowledge that because we are in His family, we will be found "not guilty" at the end of time (1 Thessalonians 1 v 9–10). It's awesome!

But there are many in the world — many people in our schools, workplaces and families — who don't follow Jesus. What will happen to them?

THE BAD NEWS

Ignoring Jesus is serious. More serious than we can ever begin to imagine. And when people live life their own way and don't ask Jesus to forgive them, they are in big trouble. On Judgment Day, everything that everyone has thought, said or done will become public — every careless word they've ever spoken (Matthew 12 v 36), every sin they've committed in private (Romans 2 v 16) will be revealed. Can you imagine how long the list of sins for each person will be? Even the most respectable-looking human being will be shown to have a huge catalogue of rebellion in their life. And God won't just say "that doesn't matter".

There are only 2 choices for human beings: either they have to let Jesus take the punishment they deserve or they have to take it themselves. People who choose not to follow Jesus, choose to take the punishment they deserve for all the times they have ignored God (2 Thessalonians 2 v 9–10).

And the Bible is clear that no one can say: "But I didn't know". Just by looking at the world, we can get a sense that God is real and important (Romans 1 v 20). And most people — whatever religion they were taught as a child — have access to the gospel. Ignoring Jesus will have massive consequences and there are no get-out clauses.

THE PUNISHMENT

Those consequences are what the Bible calls "hell": a place where people who have chosen not to follow Jesus will be punished for eternity. Hell is described in shocking ways — a place where unbelievers will be "tormented with burning sulphur" (Revelation 14 v 9–11), in a "lake of fire" (Revelation 20 v 15), in ways that produce much "weeping" (Matthew 13 v 42). Hell is endless separation from God.

The Bible's description is so shocking that some people try to pretend that it won't really happen: they suggest that God will either forgive everyone or just put them to sleep after a bit of punishment. But that's not what the Bible says. God takes sin very seriously

and the punishment for sin is serious too.

SO WHAT?

So how should we respond? If you're not a Christian or you're not sure — talk to God about it. Ask Him to rescue you. And tell a Christian who you trust.

If you follow Jesus, you can first of all praise Him for saving you from all that pain. His death and resurrection spares us from hell. And that is an amazing, undeserved truth for which to thank Him!

But there's another good way to respond too. When Paul thought about non-Christians, he was filled with "sorrow and unceasing anguish" (Romans 9 v 2). When we think about people we love going to hell, our hearts should break. And, like Paul, we can let that motivate us to tell them about Jesus and His great news of salvation.

43 | 2 Chronicles: It's a king thing

Back to 2 Chronicles' tales of the kings of Judah. It's now nearly 100 years since Solomon died. Next up as Judah's king is Asa's son, Jehoshaphat. As one of Chronicles' favourite characters, he gets a phat four chapters.

👁 Read 2 Chronicles 17 v 1–6

ENGAGE YOUR BRAIN

▶ What did the new king do to protect Judah? (v1–2)

▶ Why was God with Jehoshaphat? (v3–4, 6)

▶ What did this result in? (v5)

What a great start for Jehoshaphat. He walked God's way so God was with Him. His heart was devoted to God's ways and this was shown by the action he took (v6).

GET ON WITH IT

▶ Is your heart devoted to God's ways?

▶ Do people around you notice you're devoted to God?

▶ How should your devotion be shown by the way you live?

▶ What specifically will you change?

👁 Read verses 7–19

▶ What great thing did Jehoshaphat do? (v7–9)

▶ Why did other nations not attack Judah? (v10)

▶ What did they do instead? (v11)

King Jehoshaphat ordered a nationwide programme of education. But the focus wasn't on math or science — their textbook was God's Book of the Law. They studied God's word to learn how to live. The most important education of all is learning to live God's way.

PRAY ABOUT IT

Thank God that He teaches us so much through His word, the Bible. Pray that you'll be hungry to learn from it and put it into practice.

→ TAKE IT FURTHER

Previously in 2 Chronicles... see page 118.

44 | Truth or dare

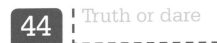

Jehoshaphat, king of Judah, loves God and serves Him. Ahab, king of Israel, doesn't. He's a nasty piece of work. So surely these two kings would be at war or at least stay away from each other. Well, no actually...

👁 Read 2 Chronicles 18 v 1–27

ENGAGE YOUR BRAIN

▶ What mistakes did Jehoshaphat make? (v1, 3)
▶ What good thing did he do? (v4)
▶ Why was Ahab reluctant? (v7)
▶ What did Ahab's prophets advise? (v10–11)
▶ Why wouldn't Micaiah just agree with them? (v13)
▶ What was God's message to Ahab? (v16)
▶ Why had the other prophets disagreed? (v22)
▶ How was Micaiah's message received? (v23–26)

▶ How did God's word come true?
▶ What lesson did God teach Jehoshaphat? (v2)
▶ What's the verdict on Jehoshaphat? (v3)

We won't always like God's message, but there's no escaping it. God always keeps His promises and we ignore them at our peril. And whatever we do in life, to do it well means obeying God and speaking the truth.

GET ON WITH IT
▶ How can you speak God's truth more and not just say what pleases people?

PRAY ABOUT IT
Ask God to help you be wise about who you hang out with and who influences you. Pray that you will speak God's truth and not just go along with the crowd.

It's not easy telling people the truth. A Christian who wants to be true to the Bible will sometimes have to say stuff people won't like. The message of Jesus often brings out anger and opposition. But God is on our side, helping us share difficult truths.

👁 Read 18 v 28 – 19 v 3

▶ What precautions did Ahab take?

→ TAKE IT FURTHER
More about evil Ahab on page 118.

45 : Turn back time

Jehoshaphat had started on the right track as king, serving God. But then he'd allied himself with godless King Ahab of Israel. Would he now listen to God's warnings and lead God's people to walk God's way?

👁 Read 2 Chronicles 19 v 4–11

ENGAGE YOUR BRAIN

▶ How did the king make sure his people turned back to God? (v4)

▶ What orders did he give his judges? (v9–10)

▶ Why was it so important that they were fair? (v6–7)

It was so vital to Jehoshaphat that the people of Judah served God. So he personally toured the country to convince them to turn back to God.

👁 Read 2 Chronicles 20 v 1–13

▶ What threat appeared on the horizon? (v1–2)

▶ What did the king do? (v3–4)

▶ What did He remember about God? (v6–7)

▶ What did he admit and what did he ask for? (v12)

Walking God's way means turning to Him first when trouble is brewing.

👁 Read verses 14–30

▶ How did God answer His people? (v15–17)

▶ How did they respond? (v20–21)

▶ What happened? (v22–28)

▶ What was the result of God's action? (v29, 30)

GET ON WITH IT

▶ Do you need to turn back to God?

▶ What do you need to remember about Him?

▶ What situation do you need God's help with?

▶ What will you praise Him for?

Take these issues to God as you pray right now.

→ TAKE IT FURTHER

Turn back to page 118.

46 Bad kings; great God

David and Solomon were far from perfect, but under their rule God's people knew God's blessing. And God showed His incredible commitment to His people by promising that a king on David's throne would rule for ever.

👁 Read 2 Chron 20v31 – 21v3

ENGAGE YOUR BRAIN

▶ *How is Jehoshaphat's reign summed up? (v32–33)*

Like his father, Jehoshaphat lived God's way. But he didn't stop all the bad stuff going on, and he made peace with the evil kings of Israel. We must be careful not to compromise when it comes to sin. If we let a little bit in, it can eventually take over.

👁 Read 2 Chron 21 v 4–11

▶ *What was Jehoram like? (v4–6)*

▶ *Why didn't God wipe out Jehoram and his family? (v7)*

Jehoram led the people of Judah away from God (v11). Yet the Lord remembered His covenant with David and didn't destroy despicable Judah. God would protect David's line of kings. Centuries later, David's greatest descendant, Jesus, would be the greatest King ever.

👁 Read verses 12–20

▶ *What was Elijah's letter about? (v12–13)*

▶ *How did God punish Jehoram and the people of Judah?*

▶ *What did the people think of Jehoram? (v19–20)*

God hates sin and will punish those who refuse to turn back to Him. Yet He also sent Jesus to offer us the chance to have our sins forgiven.

PRAY ABOUT IT

Thank God that, despite our sin and disobedience, He still loves us and sent Jesus to be the perfect King.

→ TAKE IT FURTHER

No *Take it further* today.

47 | Wicked Queen of the North

King Jehoshaphat (mostly good) and King Jehoram (completely bad) are both dead. Next to be king of Judah is Ahaziah. Watch out for his ruthless mother.

👁 **Read 2 Chronicles 22 v 1–9**

ENGAGE YOUR BRAIN

▶ *Jehoram had murdered all of his brothers. What happened to most most of his sons? (v1)*

▶ *Why did Ahaziah ignore God? (v3, 4)*

▶ *Who was behind his downfall? (v7)*

▶ *What was the situation in Judah at the end of his reign? (v9)*

Ahaziah's mother, Athaliah, was the daughter of evil King Ahab and was just like him. She led her son in evil, godless ways. And after Ahaziah's death, she got even worse.

👁 **Read verses 10–12**

▶ *What did Athaliah do? (v10)*

▶ *Any idea why?*

▶ *What secret was hidden in the temple? (v12)*

Athaliah was a real life Wicked Queen. She followed in her family's footsteps by murdering all her rivals so her position as ruler was safe. Things were looking bad for God's people in Judah. What had happened to God's promise to David that his family would continue to rule?

Things were looking bad, but God was still in control — as we'll see tomorrow. The family line of David was reduced to one kid kept hidden for six years from a murderous queen. But the family line continued: God was keeping His promise.

PRAY ABOUT IT

Thank God that we can trust Him in dark times. Pray that you won't doubt Him or turn from Him when you don't understand why things happen the way they do. God is in control.

➡ **TAKE IT FURTHER**

An alternative view on page 118.

48 ¦ Kid for king ¦

Wicked Queen Athaliah had seized power and murdered all of her rivals. All except little Joash, who was hidden in the temple until he was seven. Then Jehoida the priest decided it was time for action. Brace yourselves.

👁 Read 2 Chronicles 23 v 1–15

ENGAGE YOUR BRAIN

▶ What did Jehoida realise must happen? (v3)

▶ How was Joash protected? (v7)

▶ What controversial thing did Jehoida organise? (v11)

▶ What two things did he give young Joash?

▶ How did Athaliah react? (v12–13)

▶ What happened to her? (v15)

👁 Read verses 16–21

▶ What important thing did the people do? (v16)

▶ What else? (v17)

▶ How was Judah transformed? (v21)

Brilliant. Evil Athaliah was ousted, 7-year-old Joash was made king, and the people of Judah committed themselves to living God's way. They also destroyed everything related to worshipping idols. Turning back to God means fully committing yourself to Him and kicking out anything that gets in the way.

GET ON WITH IT

▶ Do you need to re-commit yourself to God?

▶ What "idols" do you need to throw out of your life?

PRAY ABOUT IT

Talk to God about your commitment to Him and any idols in your life.

➔ TAKE IT FURTHER
More on page 118. No kidding.

49 | From good to bad

Thanks to Jehoida the priest, Joash became king of God's people, Judah, when he was only 7. Also thanks to Jehoida, God's people are turning back to the Lord. For now.

👁 Read 2 Chronicles 24 v 1–16

ENGAGE YOUR BRAIN

▶ *What happened while Jehoida was alive? (v2)*

▶ *What did Joash want to do? (v4)*

▶ *Why was this necessary? (v7)*

▶ *How successful was the fundraising? (v10–11)*

▶ *How did the project work out? (v13–14)*

Joash repaired God's temple and things were going great. Until God-serving priest Jehoida died.

👁 Read verses 17–27

▶ *What happened? (v17–18)*

▶ *What chance did the people have to turn back to God? (v19)*

▶ *And what did they do to God's messenger? (v20–22)*

▶ *How was Judah punished? (v23–25)*

Under the brilliant influence of Jehoida, Joash had served God and the people of Judah had too. But they soon turned away from the Lord. It's predictable but tragic.

GET ON WITH IT

▶ *If things are going well with you, what might mess up your relationship with God?*

▶ *What can you do to stop this happening?*

▶ *If things are going badly, what do you need to do?*

▶ *What can you ask God?*

Talk to God openly about this stuff.

→ TAKE IT FURTHER

Sweet and sour — page 119.

50 | Another fine mess

Who's next? Step forward King Amaziah. Get ready for executions, an ill-advised war and a story about trees and thistles.

👁 **Read 2 Chronicles 25 v 1–16**

ENGAGE YOUR BRAIN

▶ How would you describe this king? (v2)

▶ What good stuff did he do? (v4)

▶ What mistake did he make? (v6)

▶ Why was this a problem? (v7–8)

▶ What happened? (v10, 13)

▶ How did the battle go? (v11–12)

▶ What went wrong? (v14–16)

Amaziah wanted to serve God but he was half-hearted. He listened to God's messengers sometimes but ignored them at others. Eventually he started worshipping idols. Uh oh. God won't stand for this.

👁 **Read verses 17–28**

▶ What did King Jehoash think of Amaziah and his army? (v18–19)

▶ Why did Amaziah fight Israel anyway? (v20)

▶ What happened to Judah? (v22–24)

▶ And to King Amaziah? (v27)

Of course Amaziah failed. Picking a fight with a much stronger enemy only works if God is on your side. But Amaziah had turned to fake gods, so the Lord let Judah get crushed. We can't expect to have God on our side if we turn from His ways. Yet God blesses those who put Him first.

PRAY ABOUT IT

Ask God to help you stick with Him in loving obedience. Pray that you'll never be tempted to turn away.

➔ **TAKE IT FURTHER**

Get the message on page 119.

51 | Loud and proud

The current pattern for kings of Judah seems to be:
1) Start well, obeying God. 2) Turn away from God,
mess up, downfall. Will King Uzziah stick to the
tragic pattern or will he buck the trend?

Read 2 Chronicles 26 v 1–5

ENGAGE YOUR BRAIN

- How did Uzziah start off? (v4)
- Who influenced him? (v5)
- What was the secret of his success? (v5)

A great start for the teenage king.
He served God, seeking Him and the
Lord gave him great success. Uzziah's
friend Zechariah helped him to live
God's way.

GET ON WITH IT

- Who can you get to teach you and help you serve God?
- Who can you help out?

Read verses 6–15

- What good stuff did Uzziah do?

God helped His king to be incredibly
successful. But...

Read verses 16–23

- What are the dangers of great success? (v16)

- What did proud Uzziah do wrong? (v18)
- What were the results of pride?
  v19–20:
  v21:
  v23:

Even though it was God who gave
him success, Uzziah became proud
and thought he could do whatever he
wanted, even ignoring God's laws. Big
mistake. And the Lord made him pay
for it. Never forget who's in control
and who is behind any success you
have. Avoid pride and make sure God
gets the glory.

PRAY ABOUT IT

Praise God for any success He's given
you. Pray that you won't become
proud and take Him for granted. Ask
Him to give you a friend who will help
you live for God.

→ TAKE IT FURTHER

Head to Isaiah for more about Uzziah.
Page 119.

52 | Good king, bad king

The next two kings break the pattern of starting off well and then going bad. This is good news for King Jotham but very bad news for King Ahaz.

👁 Read 2 Chronicles 27 v 1–9

ENGAGE YOUR BRAIN

- ▷ What's the good news and bad news in v2?
- ▷ What good stuff did Jotham do? (v3–5)
- ▷ Why was he so powerful? (v6)

👁 Read 2 Chronicles 28 v 1–4

- ▷ How bad was King Ahaz?

👁 Read verses 5–15

- ▷ How did God punish Ahaz? (v5–6)
- ▷ What did Israel do to Judah? (v8)
- ▷ What was God's message to Israel? (v9–11)

God spoke to the northern kingdom of Israel, saying: "Ease off my people in Judah". Israel listened, realised they'd done wrong and repented.

THINK IT OVER

- ▷ What sin is God challenging you about at the moment?
- ▷ How will you respond?

👁 Read verses 16–27

- ▷ Why were King Ahaz and Judah suffering? (v16–18)
- ▷ Where did Ahaz turn for help? (v16)
- ▷ What was the result? (v20–23)

Ahaz turned away from the God-serving ways of his ancestors and worshipped false gods. And in panic he turned not to God, but to evil superpower Assyria. He even gave the king of Assyria treasures from God's temple. This was a sad day in Judah's history. It would now be a servant-state of Assyria.

PRAY ABOUT IT

Turn to God now with anything that's worrying you at the moment. Pray that you'll put Him first, not letting other relationships become more important to you.

→ TAKE IT FURTHER

More from Isaiah on page 119.

53 | Heroic Hezekiah

Next up as Judah's king? Meet golden boy Hezekiah, presented as the greatest king since David and Solomon 250 years earlier. He's not without his faults, but look at his priorities...

👁 Read 2 Chronicles 29 v 1–11

By the time Hezekiah became king, the northern kingdom, Israel, had been destroyed by the war machine, Assyria, which was now set on pulverising tiny Judah too. So Hez would set about beefing up his army first, right?

- ▶ *Instead, what's he up to? (v3–5)*
- ▶ *What did Hez recognise about Judah? (v6–9)*
- ▶ *So what did he resolve to do? (v10–11)*

King Hezekiah realised that God's people had turned away from Him. So, first things first: restoring the worship and obedience of God.

👁 Skim read verses 12–28

- ▶ *What did Hezek make sure happened? (v16)*
- ▶ *Why do you think he did this?*
- ▶ *What else did he order? (v24)*

👁 Read verses 29–36

- ▶ *What else happened? (v29–31)*

- ▶ *What had Hez achieved? (end of v35)*
- ▶ *What was the mood of the people? (v36)*

The mighty and terrifying Assyrians had destroyed Israel, so surely tiny Judah needed to get ready to defend its territory. But Hezekiah saw a much greater need — the people must turn back to God, living for Him and worshipping Him in the proper way.

THINK IT OVER

- ▶ *What's worrying you at the mo?*
- ▶ *What needs do you have?*
- ▶ *But what's more important than those things?*
- ▶ *How do you need to follow Hezekiah's example?*

PRAY ABOUT IT

Ask God to sort out your priorities so you put Him first — worshipping Him with your whole life.

→ TAKE IT FURTHER

More about Hez on page 120.

54 Great invitation

The Assyrians are conquering every nation in their path. They've already destroyed Israel — surely Judah will be next. But King Hezekiah doesn't seem worried: he's more concerned that the people turn back to God.

👁 Read 2 Chronicles 30 v 1–9

ENGAGE YOUR BRAIN

▶ What did Hez want the people of Judah to do? (v1) Why? (v6)

▶ How should they be different from their ancestors? (v7–8)

▶ What would happen if they turned back to God? (v9)

However badly we've treated God, we can still turn back to Him! If we do, He'll turn back to us (v6), He'll turn His anger away from us (v8) and He'll show us great compassion (v9).

👁 Read verses 10–20

▶ What were the different responses to the orders?(v10–12)

▶ What happened to the people who hadn't purified themselves? (v18–20)

Many people refused to celebrate the Passover, but many others really wanted to worship God. Some of them broke God's laws in doing so, but Hezekiah prayed and the

Lord didn't punish them. Faith and obedience and seeking God are more important than rituals.

👁 Read 30 v 21 – 31 v 1

▶ How would you describe the relationship between God and His people? (v26–27)

▶ After celebrating Passover, what did the people do? (31 v 1)

Turn back to God and He'll show you compassion. Cry out to God and He'll answer your prayers. And if you're serious about turning to Him, you'll kick out the bad stuff in your life.

GET ON WITH IT

▶ What response do you need to make to God today?

▶ What specifically will you do?

Spend some serious time talking things over with God and thanking Him for all He's done for you.

→ TAKE IT FURTHER

Pass over to page 120.

55 | Supporting God's work

Hezekiah is leading the people of Judah back to God. He's brought proper worship back to God's temple and got the people celebrating Passover again. What next, Hez?

👁 Read 2 Chronicles 31 v 2–8

ENGAGE YOUR BRAIN
- ▶ What did the king order? (v2)
- ▶ How was it paid for? (v3)
- ▶ How were the priests and Levites to be supported? (v4)
- ▶ What brilliant thing happened? (v5–7)
- ▶ How did Hez respond? (v8)

Not only did Hezekiah encourage the people to worship God and celebrate Passover, he made sure it was an ongoing thing. Devotion to God isn't a one-off or once-a-year thing. It's daily. And it involves giving generously. And these guys gave incredibly generously to God's work!

GET ON WITH IT
- ▶ What do you currently give to God's work?
- ▶ What will you now start giving?
- ▶ How else can you support God's work at church, in the community and overseas?

👁 Read verses 9–21
- ▶ What was the great news from the chief priest? (v10)
- ▶ Who benefitted from these gifts? (v15–19)
- ▶ How is Hez described? (v20–21)
- ▶ What was the outcome? (end of v21)

This section isn't exactly packed with excitement — it's full of logistics and organisation. The Christian life isn't always exciting, and serving God often involves lots of planning and organisation. It may seem dull and take time, but it's all part of being faithful to God.

PRAY ABOUT IT
Ask God to help you give generously to His work and to serve Him faithfully even when it takes time or seems boring.

Tomorrow: the Assyrians invade!

→ TAKE IT FURTHER
Supporting programme on page 120.

56 | Terrifying enemy

The powerful Assyrian army has already destroyed the kingdom of Israel. And now it's waiting to pounce on tiny Judah. Will King Hezekiah be scared? Will he give up or stand up to this terrifying enemy?

👁 Read 2 Chronicles 32 v 1–8

▶ *What was Sennacherib's plan? (v1)*

▶ *How did Hez respond? (v2–5)*

▶ *What great encouragement did he give? (v7–8)*

Nothing and no one is more powerful than God! Never forget it.

👁 Read verses 9–23

▶ *How did Sennacherib try to terrify the people of Judah? (v10–15)*

▶ *What did Hezekiah do? (v20)*

▶ *What did God do? (v21–23)*

Sennacherib insulted God and boasted of his own achievements, but it was all part of God's plan. God would save His people and restore His honour. The Lord showed the Assyrians exactly who was boss by wiping out thousands of them, including this terrible king.

👁 Read verses 24–33

▶ *What was the good/bad/good news? (v24–26)*

▶ *Why was Hez so wealthy? (v29)*

▶ *How is his reign as king summed up? (v30)*

▶ *But what? (v31)*

Hezekiah didn't always trust God fully. And one day, God's judgment would fall on Judah for rejecting Him. Hezekiah hadn't changed people's hearts, but merely postponed God's judgment. 2 Chronicles is building to a grim climax...

PRAY ABOUT IT

Thank God that He is more powerful than anything that scares you. Pray that you would trust Him completely.

→ TAKE IT FURTHER

More about Hez on page 120.

57 | Man monster

Any idea which king of God's people reigned the longest? David? Solomon? Actually, it was Manasseh. So, he must have been the most loyal, God-serving king, right? Wrong. Look how his reign began...

👁 Read 2 Chronicles 33 v 1–9

ENGAGE YOUR BRAIN

▶ What was so bad about Manasseh? (v2–6)

▶ What was the privilege and responsibility of God's people? (v7–8)

▶ But how did they act? (v9)

Criminal: in the exact place where God shared His presence with His people, Manasseh set up an idol (v7). Manasseh's rule was a bad influence on God's people (v9). They became worse than the godless nations God had wiped out around them!

👁 Read verses 10–20

▶ How did God get the attention of a king who ignored Him? (v11)

▶ What did King Man' admit? (v13)

▶ How did he show he'd changed? (v14–16)

The people of Judah still didn't fully turn back to God. They tried to mix worship of God with bits of other religions (v17). As if God wouldn't mind. They'd soon find out the truth.

👁 Read verses 21–25

▶ What was Amon's biggest error? (v23)

2 Chronicles is building up to God's explosive judgment in chapter 36.

What lessons are there for us from this chapter? Well, no one's too far gone in sin to be out of God's reach. Past sins needn't wreck our future: Jesus offers us a way back to God. So confess the sin and get back to walking God's way.

PRAY ABOUT IT

Anything you need to say to God?

→ TAKE IT FURTHER

Big turnaround on page 120.

58 The lost book

King Manasseh sank God's people to new depths, but Judah was already a nation with judgment hanging over it. And the next king? Well, it's an eight-year-old called Josiah. What could he possibly do?

👁 Skim read 2 Chron 34 v 1–13

ENGAGE YOUR BRAIN

▶ What's the verdict on Josiah? (v2)

▶ What happened when he was 16? (v3)

▶ And when he was 20? (v3–7)

▶ And when he was 26? (v8)

👁 Read verses 14–33

▶ What did Hilkiah find? (v14)

▶ What effect did God's book have on King Josiah? (v19)

▶ Why? (v20–21)

▶ What was the message from God? (v24–25)

▶ What was the good news for Josiah? (v27–28)

After reading God's law, Josiah realised the people of Judah had turned away from God and would be punished. God's word is often not easy to swallow. It can cause distress, show up our sin and require big changes.

Josiah's response was the right one — saddened by sin, but willing to accept God's punishment and to ask Him how to make things right. If God's word challenges us that we've been disobeying Him, then we must kick out all the stuff in our lives that tempts us to sin (as Josiah did with all the idols in Judah).

PRAY ABOUT IT

Think how you can be more like Josiah as you talk to God right now. Perhaps God's showing you areas in your life that need to be dealt with. Talk to Him about that.

THE BOTTOM LINE

Gods' word should affect us deeply.

→ TAKE IT FURTHER

The book stops here — page 121.

59

The last great king?

When King Josiah discovered the book of God's law, it blew his mind. He realised the people needed to turn back to God: so he destroyed idols, repaired the temple and called for a huge feast.

👁 Read 2 Chronicles 35 v 1–19

ENGAGE YOUR BRAIN

▶ *What did Josiah do to make sure the Passover feast was celebrated properly?*
v2:
v3:
v7:

▶ *What's the verdict on this feast? (v18)*

The Passover feast celebrated God rescuing His people from Egypt centuries earlier. Moving forward with God involves remembering what He's done for you in the past. This will spur us on to keep living God's way.

THINK IT OVER

▶ *What has God done for you in the past?*
▶ *How can you make sure you remember this more often?*
▶ *How can you give generously to God's work, as Josiah and his friends did?*

👁 Read verses 20–27

▶ *Why was it foolish of Josiah to fight the Egyptians? (v21)*

▶ *What was the outcome? (v22–24)*

▶ *Yet what is King Josiah remembered for? (v26)*

It's understandable that Josiah led his army in battle against Egypt. But the Lord was actually using the Egyptian army. Josiah was offered a way out but ignored the warning and suffered God's punishment. And with that, the last great king of God's people died. Well, the last great king until Jesus — God's perfect King.

PRAY ABOUT IT

Thank God for specific things He's done for you. Pray that you will continue to walk His way. Thank Him for sending His perfect King, Jesus.

→ TAKE IT FURTHER

Jump to Jeremiah on page 121.

60 | Judah in ruins

Judah's last four kings reigned for just 22 years in total and were a godless disaster. During three of their reigns, Judah was invaded. And the final king sparked God's devastating judgment.

👁 Read 2 Chronicles 36 v 1–14

ENGAGE YOUR BRAIN

▶ *What happened to Josiah's son? (v2–3)*

▶ *What was Jehoiakim like? (v5)*

▶ *So what happened to him? (v6)*

▶ *What about his son? (v9–10)*

▶ *What outrageous things occurred during Zedekiah's reign?*
v12:
v13:
v14:

👁 Read verses 15–23

▶ *Even at this stage, what was still possible? (v15)*

▶ *But what happened? (v16)*

▶ *What finally happened to God's people? (v17–20)*

▶ *Why was that not the end for God's people? (v22–23)*

The blast of God's judgment left Jerusalem a smoking ruin, its temple trashed and its people slaves in a foreign land. But Chronicles shows us hope beyond the horror. Verse 21 says Judah was just "resting"; the temple would be rebuilt (v23); and a return would happen.

It *wasn't* over between God and His people. After 70 years, He did bring them back from exile. He does, He did, He will keep His promises.

Well done for getting through 2 Chronicles. Notice how severe God's judgment is. Notice His great mercy. Notice His promises. And recall the way back to His blessing — living God's way.

→ TAKE IT FURTHER
Final look at 2 Chron — page 121.

61 Psalms: Shout out to God

Time for a psalm. This one's entirely devoted to praising God. There's no asking God for help, no confession, depression or confusion. It's a neat reminder for us that God is always worth singing and shouting about.

👁 Read Psalm 146 v 1–4

ENGAGE YOUR BRAIN

▶ What big claim does this psalm writer make? (v2)

▶ Could you say the same? Really?

▶ Why shouldn't we put our trust in people? (v3–4)

▶ So who should we trust?

👁 Read verses 5–10

▶ Why can we trust in God?
v6:
v7:
v8:
v9:
v10:

By the way, "Jacob" (v5) and "Zion" (v10) are Old Testament names for God's people. The Lord has always looked after them and always will. God especially takes care of less fortunate people.

This is a God worth trusting. After all, He created everything and is always faithful to His people. Human beings will let us down sometimes, but the Lord never will. The God of the Bible is the only God and no one can overthrow Him. So give Him what He deserves (v10).

PRAY ABOUT IT

Well, go on then. Look back at v1–2 to help you. And if you can't honestly say those words, ask God to blow your mind again with just how much He's worth shouting about.

THE BOTTOM LINE

Praise the Lord as long as you live.

→ TAKE IT FURTHER

Prayer pointers on page 121.

62 ⌐ Raise the praise ⌐

PTL! "Praise the Lord!" Ever wondered what praising the Lord actually means? Think of it as advertising God — telling others about God so they'll know how great He is and praise Him, too.

👁 Read Psalm 147 v 1–11

ENGAGE YOUR BRAIN

▶ What are God's people expected to do? (v1)

▶ What are some of the reasons given here for praising God?

▶ What does it please God to do? (v8–9)

▶ But what does He particularly enjoy? (v11)

THINK IT OVER

▶ How can you put v11 into action?

Verse 11 is amazing. God delights in people — even sinful, selfish people who (if we're honest) rarely delight in Him.

👁 Read verses 12–20

These verses are directed specifically at God's people — those who trust and rely on Him.

▶ What special blessings did God's Old Testament people enjoy? (v12–14, v19–20)

God's word is powerful — see what it can do (v15–18). It's incredible that He should reveal it to people. And what a responsibility it gives His people to live in line with that word.

GET ON WITH IT

Stop to think about how you might praise God.

▶ How could you advertise Him more to your friends?

▶ Why not learn v11 by heart?

PRAY ABOUT IT

Ask God to help you fear Him and trust His love. PTL.

→ TAKE IT FURTHER

Praise pointers on page 121.

TOOLBOX

Reading the Bible together

When it comes to the Bible, there's an activity which must take place before we can properly enjoy its benefits. It's called reading. Obvious, really. Because God chose written language as the main method of communicating His message to us, the Bible is, first of all, meant to be read.

GET TOGETHER

And we're not talking about reading it only on special occasions or when you need help. If you want to experience God and enjoy spiritual growth, you need to develop the reading habit. Since you're using Engage, you've hopefully already developed this habit. But there's another brilliant way we can learn God's word and grow as Christians — by studying it together.

When you're part of a group Bible study, you have the advantage of learning and gaining insights from other people. It gives you the opportunity to ask questions that have been bugging you. You can be an encouragement to others and there will be times when you need encouragement yourself.

WAYS TO GET INVOLVED

• Meet with an existing Bible study group. Ask at your church or youth group about ones that meet locally to you.

• If there isn't one near you or with people your age, set one up! Grab some friends and plan it together. Decide when and where to meet regularly. And what you will study. There are loads of good Bible study guides on particular books and subjects which you can use to help you read the Bible together.

- Ask a more mature Christian to meet with you regularly to study the Bible one-to-one. This is a great way to learn from God's word, to chat things over and to pray for each other. You may even want to offer to do this with a younger Christian, to help them grow.

BIBLE STUDY DOS AND DON'TS

Do study on your own before you meet with your group. It really helps if you've already read the Bible bits you'll be looking at together, so you're not all playing catch-up, but can get straight into digging into God's awesome word.

Don't show up without first doing your homework and praying about the group.

Do feel free to disagree with someone else's interpretation of a particular verse or Bible passage.

Don't intimidate or make other people feel inferior. If you disagree, do so in a loving and gentle way.

Don't dominate the conversation in the group. Remember, your own voice sounds better to yourself than to other people.

Do be honest as you share your experiences, questions and confusion.

Don't go for "shock value". Be sensitive to other members of your group as you open up.

Do ask questions of other group members to help them to open up and take part.

Meeting up with other Christians is a great way to learn from God's word, to encourage each other and to pray together. Try it!

63 | Mark: The end

We're nearing the end of Mark's book about Jesus. Which means we're nearing the end of Jesus' life on earth. He's been arrested and is about to face a very biased trial.

👁 Read Mark 14 v 53–59

ENGAGE YOUR BRAIN

▶ Where was Jesus taken? (v53)

▶ What did Peter do? (v54)

▶ How do we know Jesus' trial was not fair? (v55, v56, v57–59)

The Jewish leaders were determined to have Jesus killed. They gathered "witnesses" to lie about Jesus and twist His words. Even so, they couldn't find any evidence to condemn Jesus to the death sentence. But that didn't stop them.

👁 Read verses 60–65

▶ What did the high priest want Jesus to admit? (v61)

▶ How did Jesus answer? (v62)

▶ How did the leaders view Jesus' response? (v63–64)

Jesus was guilty of one thing: being the Son of God. And as He stood on trial, He pointed forward to another trial, when everyone, including His enemies, will see Him "coming on the clouds of heaven". The Jewish leaders called this blasphemy — claiming to be God's Son. But Jesus was telling the truth and they refused to believe it.

People still put Jesus on trial today — they pre-judge Him, refuse to listen to Him and dismiss Him as a fake. But one day Jesus will return as Judge (v62). And those who've rejected Him will be in serious trouble.

GET ON WITH IT

Jesus told the truth about Himself even when on trial for His life. In what situations can you stand up for the truth about Him, even when it risks rejection, unpopularity, or physical harm? Ask God to give you the courage to actually do this.

→ TAKE IT FURTHER

"Son of Man" facts on page 121.

64 Trial and error

As Jesus faces a rigged trial by the Jewish leaders, another man is put on trial just outside.

Read Mark 14 v 66–72

Three times Peter is given a chance to stand up for the truth about Jesus.

▶ *What does he do with those chances? (v68, 70, 71)*

▶ *Who is interrogating him? (v66, 69, 70)*

As Jesus stands up to the most important priest in the whole nation, Peter caves in to a servant girl and some bystanders. Peter had recently claimed he would always stand by Jesus (v31). But Jesus had known what would happen (v30).

▶ *How does Peter react when he realises what he's done? (v72)*

THINK IT OVER

We're all Peters. We all fail to stand up for Jesus. We all fail to be loyal to Him in what we say and how we live. But do we all react like Peter? He broke down in tears. He was honest about himself and what he'd done.

He didn't make excuses. He didn't convince himself it didn't matter. He wept.

And the question is: when we let Jesus down, does it affect us as deeply?

PRAY ABOUT IT

Admit to Jesus ways in which you've denied Him. Feel the pain of letting Him down. Then thank Him that He knows all your flaws, and that He still died for you.

→ TAKE IT FURTHER

The next conversation we hear between Peter and Jesus can be found on p122.

65  Bad call

It's one of the most ridiculous decisions ever.
Jesus was the perfect, holy Son of God — yet
He was sentenced to death. How could this happen?

👁 Read Mark 15 v 1–15

Three sets of people sent "the king of the Jews" (v2) to the cross. Each had a different reason.

The chief priests had no power of execution so they passed Jesus on to the Roman court, and went along to continue accusing Him (v3).

▷ *Why? (v9–11)*

They wanted to be in charge. They needed Jesus out of the way so they could keep their power.

The people

▷ *What did Pilate ask the crowd? (v12)*
▷ *What's the sensible answer?*
▷ *Why did they choose to have Jesus crucified? (v11)*

The Roman governor

▷ *What surprised Pilate about Jesus? (v3–5)*
▷ *Why did Pilate allow innocent Jesus to be crucified? (v15)*

THINK IT OVER

We don't shout "Crucify Him!" But we do often live as though Jesus doesn't exist and isn't King — we sin. And we do it for the same reasons…

When do you reject Jesus as your King because:
• you want to be in charge, not Him?
• you listen to those around you, not Him?
• you choose what's easiest, rather than obeying Him?

THE BOTTOM LINE

Sin is stupid. These people chose not to let God's loving King be part of their lives — and chose to set loose a murderer. Sin means turning away from the perfect King, choosing to mess things up. Stupid.

PRAY ABOUT IT

Anything you need to say to God right now?

→ TAKE IT FURTHER

Prophetic words on page 122.

66 | Torture

Roman governor, Pilate, gave in to the murderous Jewish leaders and the bloodthirsty crowd. He released the criminal, Barabbas, and handed Jesus over to be crucified.

👁 Read Mark 15 v 15–20

ENGAGE YOUR BRAIN

▶ Even before being given to the soldiers, how was Jesus punished? (v15)

▶ Who gathered to mock and torture Jesus? (v16)

▶ How did they mock Him? (v17–18)

▶ What else did they do? (v19)

▶ What would happen next? (v20)

After someone was given the death sentence by the Romans, soldiers were allowed to torture the criminal as much as they wanted. Jesus had already been flogged — struck with leather whips that had sharp pieces of bone or metal attached, which ripped flesh off the victim's back.

Then the soldiers tortured Jesus. They dressed Him up as an idiot-king, pretending to worship Him while beating Him and spitting in His face. Jesus looked defeated. He looked pathetic. But remember what He'd said to His disciples a week earlier.

👁 Read Mark 10 v 32–34

▶ What had Jesus predicted?

Jesus knew exactly what would happen to Him. He wasn't pathetic. He wasn't defeated. Jesus willingly accepted the torture and humiliation. He deliberately went to His death to rescue sinners like us.

But this wasn't the end for Jesus. His death was yet to come. And even that wouldn't be the end.

PRAY ABOUT IT

Spend time thanking Jesus for what He went through for you. Thank Him that He's the perfect King.

→ TAKE IT FURTHER

No Take it further today.

67 Crucified

It's time to read about the greatest injustice in history. As usual, Mark doesn't mince his words — he tells it simply and quickly.

👁 Read Mark 15 v 21–24

ENGAGE YOUR BRAIN

▶ *Who was forced to help weak, beaten Jesus?*

▶ *Why do you think Jesus refused the pain-killing drink? (v23)*

Mark's description of this terrible injustice is short and simple: "And they crucified him". That's it. No detail, no blood, gore or horror. But we know Jesus' death was painful, horrific and unjust.

👁 Read verses 25–32

▶ *What do people walking past say to Jesus? (v29–30)*

▶ *What would make them believe Jesus is the Son of God?*

▶ *What do the religious leaders say about Jesus? (v31–32)*

▶ *What would make them believe Jesus is God's King?*

But Jesus stays hanging from the cross. And these people look at Him and think: He's a loser. He clearly isn't the Son of God.

But they've totally misunderstood. It's because of who Jesus is that He stays on the cross. If He hadn't been God's Son, He'd never have let Himself be killed without a fight. If He hadn't been God's King, He wouldn't be dying to save people from God's punishment: eternal death.

THINK ABOUT IT

When you look at Jesus on the cross, do you see a loser or do you see your Lord?

PRAY ABOUT IT

Thank Jesus that, although He could have easily saved Himself from the cross, He chose not to. Thank Him for deciding to go through all this so that you don't have to.

→ TAKE IT FURTHER

More prophetic words on page 122.

68 | Why did Jesus die?

People sometimes ask: "Why did Jesus die?"
Actually, He tells us Himself.

👁 Read Mark 15 v 33–34

ENGAGE YOUR BRAIN

▶ *What's strange about what happened at the "sixth hour" (midday)? (v33)*

Centuries before, God had warned this would be a sign of His anger (Amos 8 v 9). Of course God was furious — His Son was being killed! But the great surprise of the cross is not that God was angry, but who He was angry with…

▶ *What did Jesus shout? (v34)*

"Forsaken" means "abandoned" or "deserted".

▶ *What is the dying Son of God saying about His relationship with His Father?*

The punishment of complete separation from the loving God, from all joy and hope and health, should be falling on the mocking people and gloating leaders. Instead, it's falling on God's perfect, innocent Son.

👁 Read verses 35–36

As He explained why He was dying, Jesus mentioned Eloi — God (v34). But people thought He'd said Elijah (v35). So they failed to understand why Jesus died. People still do that today. They don't listen to God's Son explaining that His death is the only way they can avoid God's punishment of being abandoned by Him for ever.

Are you listening?

PRAY ABOUT IT

The punishment should have fallen on me and you. Instead, it fell on Jesus. He offers to take your place. Have you ever asked Him to do this for you? If not, what's stopping you? If you have, when was the last time you actually thanked Him properly? Do it now!

→ TAKE IT FURTHER

A little bit more on page 122.

69 | Final breath

Jesus has been falsely condemned, tortured, beaten, mocked and nailed to a wooden cross. Finally, He breathes His last breath.

👁 Read Mark 15 v 37–38

This was monumental. Jesus Christ was dead. A temple curtain ripping seems a bit of an anti-climax. But this curtain separated the rest of the temple from its innermost part — where God was present. It was a barrier between humans and God.

▶ *Why's it brilliant that it was torn open?*

With the curtain torn, the temple wasn't needed any more. No more barrier. Anyone could come to God directly through Jesus.

Read verses 39–41

ENGAGE YOUR BRAIN

▶ *What's so great about v39?*

▶ *Who else was there as Jesus died?*

More from these women over the next two days. But for now we'll focus on the Roman centurion. Many of God's own people, the Jews, had not only rejected Jesus but sent Him to His death. Incredibly, it was a non-religious, Gentile soldier who recognised Jesus' true identity as the Son of God!

Jesus' death opened the way for anyone to be a part of God's people. Anyone could now have a direct relationship with God.

👁 Read Mark 1 v 1

Through his Gospel, Mark set out to show us that Jesus is the Son of God. Amazingly, it's in His death on a cross that we can know He's God's Son.

PRAY ABOUT IT

Thank Jesus that He died for your sin and removed the barrier so you can live with God. Ask Him to give you certainty that you're headed for perfect eternity in God's presence.

→ TAKE IT FURTHER

More ripping stuff on page 122.

70 | Risky business

Jesus is dead. So why isn't that the end of the story? And why is one of the Jewish leaders getting involved?

👁 Read Mark 15 v 42–47

ENGAGE YOUR BRAIN

▷ How do we know this top religious leader wasn't an enemy of Jesus? (v43)

Matthew's Gospel tells us that Joseph was a secret follower of Jesus.

▷ What evidence are we given that Jesus really was dead?

▷ How was Joseph taking a risk?

The last thing Pilate had done was allow innocent Jesus to be killed. And now he's surprisingly releasing Jesus' body to be buried by someone else. Highly irregular. Maybe he felt guilty for condemning an innocent man.

Joseph was taking great risks for a corpse! Surely risking everything for Jesus can't do any good now... yet Joseph still does it. And in the end, Joseph has the great privilege of his tomb being the place where Jesus rose from the dead. But he doesn't

know that as he speaks to Pilate, or lays Jesus' body to rest.

▷ How is Joseph an example of how a true follower of Jesus acts?

GET ON WITH IT

▷ What risks can you take to stand up for Jesus this week?

▷ What things can you give to serving Jesus this week — some money? Some time? Some talents? Some words?

PRAY ABOUT IT

Ask God to give you courage to take risks for Jesus.

PRAY ABOUT IT

True followers of Jesus risk everything and give everything to Him.

→ TAKE IT FURTHER

No *Take it further* section today.

71 The big finale

We've reached the end of Mark's Gospel.
And what a way to end!

Read Mark 16 v 1–8

ENGAGE YOUR BRAIN

▶ Where have we seen these women before?
(Mark 15 v 40–41, 46–47)

▶ What were they doing now? (v1)

▶ What did they expect to see? (v3)

▶ Instead, what two things did they see? (v4–5)

▶ According to the angel, why was Jesus' body missing? (v6)

▶ What did he tell them to do? (v7)

▶ What amazing news did he give them? (v7)

A cold corpse on a slab in a cold tomb. Yet Jesus was brought back from the dead. He's alive! And still is.

It was a Gentile (non-Jewish) soldier who first recognised that Jesus is the Son of God. And here it's women who are first told of Jesus' astounding resurrection. Mark's saying that, because of Jesus, God's people now have open membership. Women/men, Jews/Gentiles, you/me are all welcome and equal. There are no longer any limits.

THINK IT OVER

So their fear (v8) at the incredible work of God was right. A sense of mind-blown amazement at what Jesus the Son of God came to do. Do you respond to Jesus' death and resurrection in the same way?

PRAY ABOUT IT

Stop and thank God for what Mark's Gospel has taught you. No doubt these three women eventually got talking about Jesus. Will you?

→ TAKE IT FURTHER

Why no mention of v9–20?
Find out on page 123.

Think straight, stand firm

How do you wake up your brain in the morning? Coffee? Radio? Cold shower? Cereal? The message of 2 Peter is to switch your brain on. Urgently. Because Christians need to think straight.

Peter was one of Jesus Christ's closest friends (and writer of 1 Peter, which we looked at earlier this issue). He was also an "apostle" — someone who saw Jesus after He rose from the dead, and received personal instructions from Him. The apostles' mission was to tell people what they'd seen Jesus do and had heard Him say.

Peter was writing to Christian friends. He wanted them to get their brains into gear; to think straight. To think about what they'd already heard about Jesus from the apostles — so they knew what it meant to live as Christians. Peter wanted them to deepen their understanding of what they already knew.

Peter was worried about false teachers who called themselves Christians but were spreading dangerously wrong ideas about Christ. They were making these Christians doubt what Peter had said about Jesus, and so doubt whether God had really rescued them through Jesus' death or not.

Peter wanted his friends to think straight to stand firm. To tune their brains in to what they already knew so they wouldn't be fooled by false teachers.

So, get your double-strength coffee or whatever you need... and stay tuned. Christians need to think straight to stand firm.

72 | Everything we need

This may not be the traditional way to begin a letter, but it's a brilliant one. Peter hits us with top truths right from the start.

👁 Read 2 Peter 1 v 1–2

ENGAGE YOUR BRAIN

▶ *What two things does Peter call himself?*

▶ *How does he describe the people he's writing to? (v1)*

▶ *What can Christians have because of Jesus? (v2)*

Peter humbly calls himself a servant of Jesus. And also an apostle — one sent out by Jesus to tell others about Him. Peter wants to restore his friends' confidence in what God has done for them. They were being tempted by false teachers not to believe what he'd told them.

👁 Read verses 3–4

▶ *What else has God given Christians?*

-
-
-

Through Jesus, God gives us everything we need to live for Him. He has called Christians to serve Him and gives them the ability to do it. God has promised us perfect eternal life and even now, lives in us through His Holy Spirit.

Good, eh? From first to last, our Christian faith depends on God, not us; He's the source of our faith, motivation and the spiritual strength and ability we need to keep going.

PRAY ABOUT IT
Spend longer in prayer today. Take your time working your way through today's verses, using them to help you thank God for all He's done for you and continues to do for you.

THE BOTTOM LINE
God gives us everything we need.

→ TAKE IT FURTHER
Beginning, middle and end on page 123.

73 | Keep on running

Peter's friends are in a marathon — the Christian life. They began when they became Christians; the finish line is heaven. Peter wants his readers to break the tape having a run a good race.

👁 Read 2 Peter 1 v 5–11

Being sure of what God's done, through Jesus' death and resurrection, we should work hard at living for Jesus. As with invitations to some parties, there's a dress code for heaven. It's holiness.

ENGAGE YOUR BRAIN

▶ *What qualities does Peter say Christians should have?*

-
-
-
-
-
-
-

▶ *What will Christian runners avoid if they have these things? (v8)*

▶ *What kind of athletes are they if they don't have them? (v9)*

GET ON WITH IT

▶ *Which of these qualities do you need to work on most?*

▶ *How can you do that?*

Peter wants his readers to finish the race strongly (v10–11). The "election" in v10 isn't political: it means that God has chosen people who will live with Him for ever. Peter doesn't want His readers to be smug, but to work hard at being Christians.

▶ *What great thing will happen to them if they run well? (v11)*

PRAY ABOUT IT

Thank God for giving us all we need to finish the Christian race. And for endless forgiveness that helps us to get up when we fall down and to carry on running. Ask God to help you live out the qualities listed in verses 5–7.

→ TAKE IT FURTHER

There's no *Take it further* today.

74 | Refreshing your memory

Peter's worried that his readers will be deflected from the gospel by people spreading lies about Jesus. So now he tells us how to think straight about who's right about God.

👁 Read 2 Peter 1 v 12–15

ENGAGE YOUR BRAIN

▶ Any idea what the "things" are that Peter refers to in v12? (See v1–11)

▶ What is Peter determined to do before he dies? (v13–15)

Peter knows he's going to die soon — and after he's gone, he wants his friends to think straight. To remember Jesus' rescue (v11). And to stand firm in their faith (v12). But why should we listen to Peter?

👁 Read verses 16–18

▶ So why should we listen to Peter and the other apostles? (v16)

Christianity is based on what eye-witnesses saw and heard. The apostles saw it all themselves, so what they've written (the New Testament) is reliable.

▶ How does this give you confidence when people say your faith is a load of rubbish?

👁 Read verses 19–21

▶ What should we do with the Old Testament ("word of the prophets")? (v19)

▶ Why? (v20–21)

So Jesus' rescue through His death is a historical event — Old Testament prophets predicted it and the New Testament apostles proclaimed it.

THINK IT OVER

▶ How will this knowledge help you think straight and keep going as a Christian?

PRAY ABOUT IT

Thank God that the Bible is Him speaking directly to us. Pray that you will learn from it, remember it and grow in your faith.

→ TAKE IT FURTHER

Refresh your memory on page 123.

75 | Religious conmen

Fake life insurance policies end in tears because they don't deliver what they promise. But (eternal) life insurance offered by Peter and the apostles does deliver because they're telling the truth — as we saw last time.

In chapter 2, Peter warns against conmen — and tells us what happens to people who offer false hope.

👁 **Read 2 Peter 2 v 1–3**

ENGAGE YOUR BRAIN

▶ *How are Peter's readers in the same situation as God's Old Testament people? (v1)*

▶ *What's the sad truth? (v2)*

People will always be gullible and truth will remain under threat. These conmen denied *"the sovereign Lord who bought them"*. That's Jesus, who bought them with His life when He paid for their sins on the cross. These conmen called themselves Christians, but had turned their backs on Jesus. They were in it for the money.

👁 **Read verses 4–10**

The destruction of the world by the flood and the rescue of Noah, the burning of Sodom, and the rescue of Lot all happened in Old Testament times. But what have they got to do with these religious conmen?

▶ *How does the Old Testament show what will happen to such conmen? (9–10)*

False teachers can be subtle and not always easy to spot. But the con is revealed when someone contradicts what the Bible says about Jesus. God will punish such conmen. And He'll rescue His faithful people (v9).

PRAY ABOUT IT

Ask God to help you to know the Bible better so you'll be more able to think straight and stand firm for Jesus.

➔ **TAKE IT FURTHER**
More about mysterious verse 4 on page 123.

76 | Washed pigs

Peter's warning his friends about religious conmen — false teachers who lead people away from Christ. Peter has strong words for those kind of people.

👁 Read 2 Peter 2 v 10–16

ENGAGE YOUR BRAIN

▷ *Do they know what they're talking about? (v12)*

▷ *How are they described? (v13–15)*

▷ *What will happen to them? (v12–13)*

Here's another way to spot false teachers — if someone's behaviour is clearly immoral, then their teaching probably isn't too great either.

👁 Read verses 17–22

▷ *How do false teachers con people?*
v18:
v19:

▷ *Why is an anti-God lifestyle not a life of freedom? (v19)*

▷ *What does Peter say about such conmen in v20–22?*

A washed pig going back to the mud — no fundamental change has occurred. True believers in God can be identified: they don't return, like conmen, to a filthy lifestyle.

SHARE IT

How will you answer people who say: "Forget old fashioned morality, no sex before marriage etc. So what if it's in the Bible? Real Christianity is about freeing the spirit"?

PRAY ABOUT IT

Think straight, or you'll be sucked into a wrong lifestyle. Ask God to help you not get conned into doubting the message of the Bible. Or conned into thinking that being free is doing what feels good at the time.

THE BOTTOM LINE

To obey God is to be really free.

→ TAKE IT FURTHER

Grab some more on page 123.

77 ¦ Jesus — the return

Ever get teased for your faith in Jesus? Peter says Christians will be taunted by unbelievers and made to question their beliefs. So think straight and stand firm.

👁 Read 2 Peter 3 v 1–2

ENGAGE YOUR BRAIN

▶ Why did Peter write his two letters? (v1)

▶ In the face of false teaching, what must his friends do? (v2)

👁 Read verses 3–7

▶ What do people try to make Christians doubt? (v4)

▶ What have they forgotten? (v5–6)

▶ And what will happen when Jesus returns? (v7)

The "last days" (v3) means the time between Jesus' return to heaven in 1st century AD and His second coming in the future. Peter's friends lived in the last days, and so do we.

People will mock us and try to make us doubt that Jesus will return. But God's word is a guarantee that it will happen. We can see from the Bible that God always keeps His promises. Jesus WILL return and take His people to a perfect new life.

👁 Read verses 8–9

▶ Why is Jesus delaying His return?

THINK IT OVER

"Repentance" (v9) = turning to Christ; becoming a Christian.

▶ What would have happened to you if Jesus had returned before you became a Christian?

▶ What will happen to your friends if they don't become Christians before Jesus returns?

PRAY ABOUT IT

Thank God that He's delaying the second coming so people have a chance to turn to Jesus. Thank Him that you had that chance. Pray for friends who don't know Jesus yet.

→ TAKE IT FURTHER

No *Take it further* today.

93

78 | Wait, watch

Listen up. Peter's got more to say on Jesus' return — and how Christians should live while we wait.

👁 Read 2 Peter 3 v 10–14

ENGAGE YOUR BRAIN

▶ *In what way will Jesus' return be like a burglary? (v10)*

▶ *What will happen to the universe when Jesus returns? (v10, 12)*

▶ *Will that be the end of everything? (v13)*

When the world ends, Christians are going to get a new "home of righteousness" — a great place with no selfishness, depression or death. A place where we'll be overcome by how great and loving God is. A place to get excited about.

▶ *So what should Christians do while we wait for this? (v11–12)*

▶ *What should we aim for?*

▶ *What do you think that means exactly?*

Peter says: "Make every effort". He doesn't say we'll always succeed at being blameless (obviously!). But he is saying don't aim for second best. Don't be half-hearted. Be in training when Jesus comes again.

GET ON WITH IT

▶ *How do you shape up alongside v14?*

▶ *What do you need to work on for starters?*

PRAY ABOUT IT

Thank God that Jesus will return one day and that believers can look forward to a perfect new world. Ask Him to help you live for Him as you wait excitedly.

THE BOTTOM LINE

Make every effort to be found spotless, blameless and at peace with Him.

→ TAKE IT FURTHER

Wait for it... more on page 124.

79 | Ready, steady, grow

Peter signs off now with a few reminders, warnings, encouragements and even some name-dropping. Ask God to speak to you through 2 Peter one more time.

👁 Read 2 Peter 3 v 15–16

ENGAGE YOUR BRAIN
▶ *What are Peter and Paul agreed on? (v15, and see v9)*

OK, so Peter didn't always find Paul easy to understand (neither will we at times!). But Paul's letters are important — God is the driving force behind them, speaking to us.

▶ *Instead, how do the conmen treat Paul's letters? (v16)*

👁 Read verses 17–18
▶ *These verses sum up Peter's letter. Try to put it into your own words:*

Peter says: "Don't get taken in by religious conmen and false teachers. Instead, grow in your faith." The way to grow is:

1. Remember that God's forgiveness and love are always there for us because of Jesus (that's grace, v18).

2. Know more and more about what it means to obey Jesus in our daily lives (that's knowledge, v18).

GET ON WITH IT
▶ *What exactly can you do to...
remember?*

know more?

obey?

PRAY ABOUT IT
Ask God to help you do this daily. And thank Him for 2 Peter.

Oh, and remember: think straight and stand firm.

→ TAKE IT FURTHER
Yep, there's more on page 124.

80 | Proverbs: Hard-hitting words

Remember King Solomon, the wisest man that ever lived? Well, God's going to talk to us through Sol's wise words in Proverbs. Brace yourself...

👁 **Read Proverbs 25 v 1–28**

and jot down any proverbs that really hit you.

Written one down? Perhaps you need to pay attention to it right now. You have our permission to ignore the rest of the page if you need to.

Wrote down more than one? Is there a link between them? What point is God's word driving home to you?

👁 **Read verses 9–10, 18, 25**

It's all too easy to be put to shame by speaking without thinking, or by defending yourself at someone else's expense (v9–10).

▶ *When have you done that recently?*

▶ *When have you slandered someone's character?*

▶ *What effect does this have? (v18)*

▶ *How is good news described? (v25)*

▶ *What good news can you give your friends?*

PRAY ABOUT IT

Talk to God about the lessons you've learned today. Ask Him to help your words build people up, not knock them down.

➔ **TAKE IT FURTHER**

More wise words about words: p124.

81 | Fool's gold

Today's wise sayings are about fools, lazy people, practical jokers, gossips and smooth talkers. Know any? Feel like you're one of those? Ask God to speak to your heart today.

👁 Read Proverbs 26 v 1–12

Fools are people who ignore wisdom and fail to take God seriously. It doesn't matter how well you do at school, if you disobey God — that's real foolishness. Living God's way is true wisdom. So anyone who reads a proverb that applies to them and refuses to change — they're a fool. So take these next proverbs seriously.

👁 Read verses 13–19

▶ *What are we told about lazy people ("sluggards")?*

▶ *In what ways are you lazy?*

▶ *How could you be a less lazy Christian?*

▶ *Ever use the phrase "Only joking!" after you deceive or hurt someone?*

▶ *Need to apologise?*

👁 Read verses 20–28

▶ *What are we told about gossip? (v20, 22)*

▶ *And about smooth talk? (v24–28)*

GET ON WITH IT

▶ *Any idea what God is saying to you today?*

▶ *So... what will you do about it?*

PRAY ABOUT IT

If God has challenged you, make sure you act on it. Right now. Don't delay. Pray for His help with what you need to do.

→ TAKE IT FURTHER

Confusing contradiction on page 124.

82 Friendly advice

What kind of friend are you? What do most of your friends have in common? The Bible says friendships are important — and who we hang out with matters.

👁 Read Proverbs 27 v 1–6

ENGAGE YOUR BRAIN

▷ Why shouldn't we boast about stuff that hasn't happened yet? (v1)

▷ What do we learn about praise? (v2)

▷ What do you think v6 means?

Who prefers wounds to kisses??? Verse 6 says that real friends should tell us the not-so-great things about us. We won't enjoy hearing them; they might wound us; but we need to hear them. If someone's all fake and only says nice stuff about us, what sort of friend are they?

👁 Read verses 7–13

▷ What are we told about friends? (v9, 10)

We shouldn't choose our friends by who says the nicest things about us. Real friends build us up but also tell us when we're going off the tracks. They give us wise (godly) advice (v9). We all need friends to encourage us and support us in the Christian life. We can't just rely on family all the time (v10). We need good Christian friends too.

THINK IT OVER

▷ Who do you need to listen to more?

▷ Who should you listen to less?

▷ Who do you need to be a better friend to?

▷ Anyone you need to talk straight (yet gently) to?

PRAY ABOUT IT

Talk to God about your friendships. And ask Him to help you take any action you need to.

→ TAKE IT FURTHER

Back to the future — page 124.

83 | Everyday proverbs

Someone smart said that Proverbs is about "godliness in working clothes" — how to live God's way in everyday life. As you read today's verses, think how they apply to you at home/school/college/work or out with friends.

Read Proverbs 27 v 14–22

ENGAGE YOUR BRAIN
▷ *Pick one of these proverbs and try to explain it in your own words. Choose from v17, 18 and 21.*

Here's what we've come up with.

v17: We should help to develop and mould each other in our faith, just as knives are sharpened by steel.

v18: Hard work and serving your boss will pay off.

v21: How we handle praise shows what we're like. Learning to handle praise without giving in to pride refines us as Christians. We become more like Jesus.

Read verses 23–27
▷ *How can we apply these verses to managing our finances?*

You might not own many sheep or goats, but the principles here are sound ones. We should be careful to wisely use the resources God gives us. Don't spend all your money at once. Make sure you clothe and feed yourself and look after your family.

GET ON WITH IT
▷ *What have you learned today?*

▷ *Gonna do anything about it?*

What do you need to talk to God about today?

→ TAKE IT FURTHER
No *Take it further* today.

99

84 Mixed bag

Today's bunch of proverbs are a mixed bag, but look out for some key themes — law and justice; money and greed; evil tyrants. Don't forget to pray before you start reading.

👁 Read verses 4–5, 7, 9–10

ENGAGE YOUR BRAIN

▶ What are we told about law-breakers?

▶ What about law-abiding citizens?

▶ What laws do you "bend"?

▶ How can you "seek the Lord" in this area?

👁 Read verses 3, 12, 16, 28

▶ What does Solomon say about wicked rulers?

▶ Which countries in the world does this make you think of?

PRAY ABOUT IT

Take time out to pray for these countries, that their evil rulers would be overthrown. Pray for Christians in these countries. Short of ideas? Try www.csw.org.uk

👁 Read verses 6. 8, 19–22, 27

▶ What do we learn here about... greed?

hard work?

generosity?

👁 Read verses 13–14

▶ What are the big lessons here?

GET ON WITH IT

Select one verse from this chapter. Learn it; seek to obey it; tell God how it affects you.

→ TAKE IT FURTHER

Mix things up on page 124.

85 Sol's smart sayings

Today is the final instalment of Solomon's proverbs — tomorrow, Agur takes over. We'll have a look at the big themes of this chapter, but watch out for the proverb that God's got in store for you today.

👁 **Read Proverbs chapter 29**

Yes, all of it. Slowly.

SPEECH

Check v5, 11, 20 and 22.

▶ *Do you need to apologise to God and ask Him for help?*

Flattery is no help to others (v5). And letting your anger out may be recommend by so-called experts but not by God. Have you taken in verses 11 and 22?

SELF-CONTROL

Look at v8, 11 and 18.

▶ *How good are you at turning away anger, at keeping yourself under control?*

▶ *Or do you just let your temper go and flip?*

Where there's no guidance from God, there's no restraint (v18). Ask God to help you live as you know He wants you to.

FAMILY LIFE

It's here in v 3, 15 and 17.

▶ *How well were you disciplined by your parents?*

▶ *Would you really have wanted to be left to yourself? (v15)*

▶ *How do you think you'll discipline your own kids if you have any?*

▶ *How much is v17 true in your family?*

IN CONTROL

See v13, 25 and 26.

It's a theme that runs through the whole book. The Lord God is in control. Over-ruling. Thank God right now for that reassurance.

PRAY ABOUT IT

Just an idea — read chapter 29 (or part of it) again and say a prayer after each verse. Be brief. Be honest.

→ **TAKE IT FURTHER**

More from Sol on page 125.

86 | Mystery man's wise words

We've read loads of Solomon's wise sayings; now it's Agur's turn. This guy is a mystery. He's not mentioned anywhere else in the Bible. All we know is that he delivered great proverbs from God. So listen up to God's mystery man.

👁 Read Proverbs 30 v 1–4

ENGAGE YOUR BRAIN

- ▶ *How does Agur describe himself? (v2–3)*
- ▶ *Who doesn't he know much about? (v3)*

Agur rightly says that God is in heaven, hidden from His creation. And he's right that our puny human minds can't possibly understand all there is to know about the Holy One — God. And yet you and I can know God more closely than Agur. Jesus' death and resurrection have made it possible for us to be friends with God. In Jesus, we can know God intimately.

👁 Read verses 5–6

- ▶ *What's another way we can learn about God? (v5)*
- ▶ *What does Agur say about God's word and about God Himself? (v5)*
- ▶ *So what should we do? (end of v5)?*
- ▶ *And what shouldn't we do? (v6)*

- ▶ *How can you take v5 to heart and act on it?*

👁 Read verses 7–9

- ▶ *What two things does Agur pray for?*
- ▶ *Why? (v9)*

This guy wants to serve God and he doesn't want anything to distract him. He prays to be kept from lies and both wealth and poverty. He knows that being rich can lead people to be self-reliant and ignore God. And he knows that being poor can lead to crime. He just wants enough to live on and to keep obeying the Lord.

PRAY ABOUT IT

- ▶ *What's good about his attitude?*
- ▶ *What similar things can you pray for yourself?*

So... get praying.

→ TAKE IT FURTHER
More wise words on page 125.

87 | Animal advice

Are you ready for some strange sayings? These ones involve swords, leeches, vultures, fire, milk, eagles, snakes and lizards. Ask God to clearly show you what He wants to say to you today.

👁 Read Proverbs 30 v 10–17

ENGAGE YOUR BRAIN

▷ How might v10 apply to workers and bosses?
▷ Which of the people in v11–14 are you most like?
▷ How can you make a real effort to change?
▷ Is the outcome good or bad for people who mock or disobey their parents? (v17)
▷ How can you work on respecting and obeying your mother/father?

👁 Read verses 18–23

▷ Who amazes and perplexes this guy? (v18–19)

He finds it difficult to understand these four "ways" because they leave no easy-to-follow tracks. But exactly what we're supposed to learn from all this is beyond my understanding! Verse 20 seems to use eating as a metaphor for sex. The person who commits adultery often thinks they're doing nothing wrong and it becomes

as natural and easy as eating.

▷ Any idea what v21–23 means?

If you do, please let us know!

👁 Read verses 24–33

▷ Which of the creatures in v24–31 can you learn from?
▷ What is God be teaching you?

By the way, a conie is a rock badger, or hyrax.

▷ How are you sometimes like v32–33?
▷ What's God's warning to you?
▷ What will you do?

PRAY ABOUT IT

Cast your eye over the chapter again, and note any ideas that strike you. Then pray for God's help to listen to Him and obey Him.

➔ TAKE IT FURTHER

No *Take it further* today.

88 | Sex, booze and justice

Time to meet another mystery man. King Lemuel doesn't feature in the history books, but his mother's great advice has been immortalised in the Bible, to be read by millions of people. So it must be good stuff...

👁 Read Proverbs 31 v 1–3

ENGAGE YOUR BRAIN
▷ *What is the king warned against?*

Lemuel's mum was worried he would be led astray by immoral women. It's the kind of thing most parents worry about — their kids getting into bad relationships.

▷ *How might such a relationship lead you away from God?*

▷ *Is this something God's warning you about?*

▷ *What do you need to do about it?*

▷ *Who will you talk to about it?*

👁 Read verses 4–7
▷ *Why shouldn't kings get drunk? (v5)*

▷ *What does Lemuel's mother say about alcohol? (v6–7)*

▷ *What do you think about that?*

Alcohol in moderation can have a relaxing effect. But too much of it can impair your decision-making and lead to bad choices and bad situations.

▷ *Do you ever drink too much?*

▷ *What effect does it have on you?*

▷ *Anything you need to do?*

👁 Read verses 8–9
▷ *How exactly can you act on this great advice?*

PRAY ABOUT IT
What has God said to you today? Talk to Him about it. Be honest and open. And keep praying that you'll actually do what He wants you to do.

→ TAKE IT FURTHER
More about alcohol — page 125.

89 It's a wonderful wife

We finish Proverbs with a poem about the perfect wife. See how it matches up to your idea of a great life partner.

ENGAGE YOUR BRAIN

Write down your top five ingredients for the perfect husband/wife:

1.
2.
3.
4.
5.

👁 Read Proverbs 31 v 10–31

Some of this will seem very strange to our culture and time. But the basic characteristics of a good companion shine through.

Write down Proverbs' top five ingredients for a marriage partner:

1.
2.
3.
4.
5.

▶ *What's the huge point made in v30?*

This poem's saying there are other things which, dare we say it, are more important than physical attraction and sex drive.

▶ *What's the vital characteristic that is at both the beginning of Proverbs (1v 7) and the end?*

Yep, fearing God was the secret to all this wife's hard work, business sense, reliability and kindness.

▶ *How do your two top five lists compare?*

▶ *Has the book of Proverbs taught you the fear of the Lord?*

▶ *Have you started to change to become more God-wise?*

PRAY ABOUT IT

Learning the fear of the Lord — living for God and trusting His word — is a job for life. Ask God to help you and thank Him for Proverbs.

→ TAKE IT FURTHER

Final wise words — page 125.

90 Psalms: Praise party

Welcome to the last 3 pages of Engage and the final 3 psalms. They encourage us to praise God and give us heaps of reasons why we should.

👁 Read Psalm 148 v 1–6

ENGAGE YOUR BRAIN

▶ Who is called to praise God in v2–4?

▶ Why should they? (v5–6)

👁 Read verses 7–14

▶ Who else is called to praise God?

There's no excuse for not giving God the praise He deserves. All of the heavens (v1–4) and all of the earth (v7–12) should be praising God. That's everyone!

▶ What reasons are given?
v13:
v14:

Praise God (v13): because He's shown us what He's like. We know His name, which tells us about His character.

Praise God (v14): because He's given His people ("saints") a king ("horn"). The New Testament shows us that

God's chosen King is Jesus — who has come to rescue His people and lead them.

We're also told that God's people are "close to His heart".

▶ How does this truth encourage you?

PRAY ABOUT IT

Maybe you've had a tough time recently. Tired? Fed up? Struggling? Worried? Or getting on OK? Psalm 148 says God should be praised — however we feel. So will you thank and praise God this very moment?

→ TAKE IT FURTHER

Party on — page 125.

91 ¦ Songs and swords ¦

This is a psalm of two halves. Two very different halves. As you read it, remember that "saints", "Zion" and "Israel" are Old Testament names for God's people.

👁 Read Psalm 149 v 1–5

ENGAGE YOUR BRAIN

▶ *What should God's people do?*

▶ *Why? (v4)*

Check out verse 2 again — not only is God the Creator, but He's made a people for Himself. He's not just *the* King, but *our* King too. He has saved us (v4). All this should get us dancing on our beds (v5)!

👁 Read verses 6–9

▶ *What's so surprising about the second half of the psalm?*

This psalm was written in Old Testament times, when God's people were a specific nation — Israel. God protected His people, and Israel was often told by God's spokesmen (prophets) that He'd take action against those who rejected His rule. So sword-talk isn't that strange; God's people are celebrating that God is just and fair. Those who reject Him will be

punished (v9). And God will use His people to do this.

In the New Testament, God's people are found in every nation. And what God said — His word — is described as a sword. So when we explain the Bible's message to people, we shouldn't just talk about God's rescue, but also mention His punishment for those who reject Him.

GET ON WITH IT

▶ *What do you know about God that's worth singing about?*

▶ *What message about God are you passing on to non-Christian friends?*

▶ *Does it include both God's love and His justice?*

PRAY ABOUT IT

Pray for those friends now.

➔ TAKE IT FURTHER

More about God's word on page 125.

 The big finish

The final song in the book of Psalms is short and sweet. No prizes for guessing it's another praise song to God. So break out your instruments and get your dancing shoes on.

Read Psalm 150

"Sanctuary" = God's temple. The one built in Jerusalem, which symbolised God living among His people. It set Him apart from them too, as He's a holy God.

ENGAGE YOUR BRAIN

▶ What two reasons are given for praising God? (v2)

▶ Can you give examples of these two things?

•

•

▶ What was used to praise God? (v3–5)

▶ Who is called to praise God? (v6)

THINK IT OVER

Have a flick back through Psalms 146–150.

▶ What is it about God that deserves praise?

▶ What has He done for you that you need to praise Him for?

▶ Can you echo Psalm 150 v 6?

In heaven, God's people — overcome with how great He is and so grateful for what He has done — will praise God for ever.

PRAY ABOUT IT
Let's get in the habit now.

→ TAKE IT FURTHER
The final word is on page 125.

TAKE IT FURTHER

If you want a little more at the end of each day's study, this is where you come. The TAKE IT FURTHER sections give you something extra. They look at some of the issues covered in the day's study, pose deeper questions, and point you to the big picture of the whole Bible.

1 PETER
Pain before gain

1 – PERFECT STRANGERS

Have you taken in what it means to be "God's elect"?

Read Ephesians 1 v 4–14

Christians have so much to thank God for. He redeemed them — bought them back from slavery to sin. It cost the life of His Son. And look what it gave us — true forgiveness. We're part of God's plan that will end in Jesus ruling over a new heaven and a new earth. One day, the whole universe will worship Jesus as King.

God chose His people from the beginning of time (v4). But it still requires us to believe that Jesus' death can save us — we must put our trust in Him (v13). Those who do are marked as belonging to God (v13). They receive His Holy Spirit, who guarantees that one day they'll receive everything God has in store for them in His new world. All of this should lead to us praising God big time (v12, v14). So why not do that right now?

2 – A NEW HOPE

Read 1 Peter 1 v 10–12

For centuries, the prophets were on the lookout for the coming Christ — the ruler sent by God who'd save people. How fortunate these Christians are that they're the ones who've been able to hear about Jesus Christ! And that goes for us too. We're no longer waiting for the Christ; we can actually get to know Him personally!

3 – LOOK AROUND YOU

Verse 16 is a quote from all sorts of places — look up **Leviticus 11 v 44–45; 19 v 1–2; 20 v 7–8**. And Jesus gives us a similar command in **Matthew 5 v 48**. Read it.

▶ Who are we to look like?
▶ Who will give us this family likeness?

Being holy means being set apart for God, who is perfect and rescues His people. Because God has rescued Christians, their lives are now His. He is holy, so they must make every effort to be holy. That doesn't mean floating around, being super-religious — it means living a life that pleases God.

109

4 – STRANGE BUT TRUE

Read verses 18–21 again

Two things to help us here:

a) In Peter's day, slaves could be given their freedom if someone *redeemed* them (paid money to buy them back).

b) In the Old Testament (see Exodus 12), the Israelites escaped from slavery in Egypt by sacrificing a lamb — a perfect one.

So, Peter says, the price has been paid to set you free. That price was the precious life of Jesus — the perfect man who gave His life as a sacrifice, like a lamb.

Spend 10 minutes thanking God that He sacrificed so much for you; and thinking about what a great future He's given you. Then see if you can spend 10 minutes being a completely self-centred ratbag. Not so easy? Get the point?

5 – MILKING IT

See how God's word is described in **Psalm 19 v 7–14**. Why not use these verses to help you pray that you would see God's word as the psalm writer does?

6 – LOVE/HATE RELATIONSHIP

Read verse 9 again

It had always been hard to get near God. Non-Jews were barred from the temple in Jerusalem. Even Jews couldn't get to its inner room, where God's presence was. Only a priest could, once a year, carrying blood, because of God's anger at sin. Now, big shock. See how Jesus has changed everything?

▶ *How does Peter describe Christians in v5, 9–10?*

Christians don't have holy buildings: they *are* a holy building, a temple, in which God lives. Christians don't need priests to meet with God on their behalf: they *are* a priesthood and can meet with God themselves. And anyone, Jew or Gentile, can now be one of God's people (v10). And these new people of God should be letting others know how great God is.

▶ *What are two ways of doing this? (v9, 12)*

▶ *What will it also involve? (v11)*

7 – GOD'S THE BOSS

Check out Philippians 2 v 5-11

Let it sink in and pray that God would help you to have the same attitude (v5).

▶ *Who is Jesus? (v6)*

▶ *What didn't He do? (v6)*

▶ *What did He do? (v7–8)*

▶ *What did God think of this? (v9)*

Jesus is worth it — He's God! But He gave up everything He deserved and was humble enough to die on a Roman cross to serve others.

▶ *So what does that mean for us? (v5)*

Here's our motto for life — not "because I'm worth it" but "my attitude should be the same as that of Christ Jesus". We live Jesus Christ's way by copying His attitude.

8 – SUFFERING SERVANT

We see the same attitude of doing good even while being treated badly throughout the Bible — not just in God's people but in God Himself. Despite all our sin and rebellion, God keeps offering us a way back, even when it is thrown back in His face time and time again. Jesus' death on the cross is the ultimate example (see Acts 2 v 22–24).

2 CHRONICLES
It's a king thing

9 – WISDOM OR WEALTH?
Read verses 3–5 again
The ark (the box containing the 10 Commandments) represented God's grace; the altar (where sacrifices were offered) symbolised man's response to God's grace. Later (chapter 5), ark and altar came together in the new temple.

**Read verse 7
and then Matthew 7 v 7–11**
Get the order right, as Sol did: trust God and He'll provide. Not: insist God provides before you trust. God's blessings for His people now are far better than a truck-load of chariots (or money). They're all to be found in Jesus: He assures us we're forgiven by God; He brings us into a lasting relationship with God; He lives in us by His Spirit; He guarantees us life in God's new world, where we'll enjoy God's blessings in full. What a prospect to hang on to!

10 – HIRAM'S HELPING HAND

God's people today don't have a temple; all that was fulfilled in Jesus, whose one sacrifice of Himself means that no further sacrifices for sin are needed.

Read Hebrews 10 v 11–14
and make a point of thanking Jesus.

11 – BEHIND THE CURTAIN
Read 2 Chronicles 4 v 1–22
The "Sea" (v2) was a huge bowl used by the priests for ceremonial washing — to make them clean enough for God.

Now read Titus 3 v 3–8
It's Jesus who now washes us clean and makes us acceptable to God. Before we became Christians, our lives were a mess. We didn't deserve anything from God, yet He mercifully rescued us from our sinful lives. He sent Jesus to die in our place so that our lives could be washed clean and renewed by the Holy Spirit. Christians are "justified" (v7) — put right with God, forgiven, accepted by Him. So they should be careful to devote themselves to doing what is good (v8).

12 – CLOUD CONTROL

This was a great moment. God's temple was complete and His ark was now in the temple. God was with His people. Awesome. And He had kept His promises to King David. Everything was looking good for God's people. For now.

God always keeps His promises. The most

incredible promise He made was to send His Son to rescue us. Jesus' death and resurrection have made it possible for us to have access to the perfect, holy God.

13 – SOL SPEAKS TO GOD
Read verses 30 & 37
▶ *What was at the heart of the human problem?*

Now read Hebrews 8 v 10–12
▶ *What's so great about the new covenant that Jesus brought?*
▶ *How can you let these awesome truths truly impact your life?*

14 – WORDS OF WARNING
Imagine you're one of the original readers of Chronicles — you're one of a struggling minority trying to keep going with God.
▶ *What's the way back?*
▶ *How, in your everyday life, can you make sure you look more to God?*
▶ *How do you need to make Him the priority in your life?*

16 – SPICE GIRL
The story of Solomon is also in 1 Kings, which is not so completely positive about Sol. Chronicles doesn't tell about Solomon turning away from God or about the enemies he made in his old age. Why not?

Well, the readers of Chronicles would have read 1 Kings and known it already. Instead, Chronicles aims to highlight the greatness of Solomon — devoting himself to leading God's people to fulfil God's

purposes — and all the good things that followed.
▶ *How might this have encouraged/ challenged the original readers?*
▶ *How should it affect us?*

OK, Sol was far from perfect, so the Bible points us to the One who'd rule God's people perfectly, for ever.

17 – TIME TO SPLIT
The kingdom split in two:
Judah in the south: 2 tribes, Jerusalem its capital, Rehoboam its king.
Israel in the north: 10 tribes, Shechem its capital (at first), Jeroboam its king.

10 v 19 sums up the next 200-ish years, until Israel suffered God's punishment when the Assyrians invaded in 722BC (Judah was later exiled in 587BC by Babylon). By the way, Chronicles uses "Israel" interchangeably to describe Israel *or* Judah. Confusing.

18 – IGNORING GOD
Want to know what was happening in the northern kingdom of Israel? Then check out **1 Kings 12 v 25 – 14 v 20**.

King Jeroboam was bad news. He broke the unity of God's people; he set up idols; he diverted people away from God's temple; he made anyone a priest, against God's law; he re-arranged God's calendar of festivals; and he took the priest's role himself. No wonder he forfeited the promise God had made to him (11 v 38).

God gave Jeroboam the chance to change his ways but, amazingly, he refused. We must be careful not to ignore God's warnings when He gives us the chance to turn back to Him.

19 – BATTLE CRY

Read 1 Kings 15 v 1–8

▶ *How does this paint a very different picture of Abijah?*

So Abijah wasn't fully devoted to God and he followed the disgusting ways of his dad, Rehoboam. Yet God kept His promise to David to keep the family line going. God always keeps His promises, no matter how bad things are.

20 – PEACE AT LAST

Read verse 7 again

Asa trusted God in the past ("we sought...") and then, at this stage, continued to do so ("let us build..."). The message is: keep going, continuing to trust God and what Jesus has done.

Someone said about following Christ: "The vital decision is not the one made yesterday or last year or 10 years ago, but the one which is made today".

▶ *Why's that?*

21 – GREAT START, TERRIBLE FINISH

It's awful to have known God and trusted Him, but then to end up angry at God, self-obsessed and self-reliant.

▶ *Are you aware of this danger?*
▶ *What will you do, with God's help, to avoid it?*

1 PETER

22 – PAIN BEFORE GAIN

Read Ephesians 5 v 21–33

▶ *What does v22 mean?*
▶ *Why must wives do this? (v24)*

Paul says marriage is a picture of Christ's relationship with His church (all Christians). Believers should adoringly give their lives to serving Jesus, accepting His authority. And wives should accept the authority of their husbands, as an expression of unselfish love. But don't assume that husbands get an easy ride...

▶ *How must husbands treat their wives? (v25, v28)*
▶ *What goals should a husband have? (v26–27)*

Husbands must show the self-giving, sacrificial love that Jesus did for His church. Their wives can become all that God wants them to be. Great, eh? A husband should love and look after His wife in the same way he cares for himself — instinctively and naturally — because she's part of him now (v31). Amazingly, Christ also counts His people as His own body and He cares for them, providing for them. Both sets of relationships are incredibly intimate.

23 – LIVING IN HARMONY

Behaviour is never a way of getting God to accept us. Take the book of Romans for example. It's only after eleven, yes, eleven chapters of telling us how God has saved us by His grace and mercy, that Paul turns to telling us how we should live as believers (check out the "therefore" at the start of chapter 12!). Our behaviour is a grateful and loving response to the God who made us and bought us by His blood — we are doubly His.

24 – STAND UP, SPEAK OUT

See what Jesus has to say about fearing men in **Matthew 10 v 28**. Pray for the right perspective on life! But also remember that one of the most frequent sayings in the Bible is "do not fear". God knows our weaknesses and our worries and is with us — read **Isaiah 41 v 10**.

25 – CHRIST'S PERFECT EXAMPLE

Read verses 19–22 again

Peter's giving reassurance to Christians who must cope with suffering and persecution. He's saying:

1) Christ conquered sin by His death and resurrection. He's brought you to God. Don't fear opposition. You belong to the God of glory.

2) By the power of the Spirit of Jesus, Noah preached to people around him, but they refused to believe. They're now "spirits in prison" — suffering God's eternal punishment. But God saved Noah and his family, so...

3) God will save us, who, through the work of the Spirit (demonstrated

in baptism) share in Jesus' death and resurrection, and who have willingly submitted ourselves to Him.

Does this help? Chew it over.

26 – LIVING FOR GOD

Look at verse 1 again

▶ *How does being prepared to suffer show that you're serious about getting rid of sin in your life?*

▶ *Can you think of sins that would be painful to cut out of your life?*

Elsewhere in the New Testament, Paul speaks about "putting to death" this way of living. Check out **Romans 8 v 12–14** and **Colossians 3 v1–10** for some encouragement to get serious.

27 – LOVE ABOVE ALL

There's a lot of talk about "gifts" or "spiritual gifts" in Christian circles, but the Bible doesn't differentiate between different sorts of gifts. Marriage is called a gift, as is singleness, hospitality, philanthropy and administration, as well as the more "exotic" ones like prophecy or speaking in tongues! Why not read **Romans 12 v 3–8, 1 Corinthians 12 v 1–13** and **Ephesians 4 v 1–13** and ask yourself the following questions:

▶ *Who are the gifts from?*
▶ *Who is gifted?*
▶ *Why are the gifts given?*

28 – PAINFUL READING

Read verse 13 again

For Christ, suffering was followed by the glory of being raised to God's right hand. Peter says that if you're suffering because you're a follower of Jesus, then be encouraged — one day you'll share in His glory too.

Most Engage readers probably have it fairly easy as Christians in the country they live in. But that's not true in every country. Why not read a book about a Christian who has had to suffer much more? Or find out if your church has links with someone living in a country where it is tough to be a Christian? It could just encourage you to be ready for anything...

29 – RELATIONSHIP ADVICE

Prayer is difficult. Sometimes we feel too sinful, too tired, too unimportant or generally too rubbish to do it. Why would God be interested in hearing from me? Learn verse 7 off by heart and remind yourself of it daily.

30 – IN CONCLUSION...

Read verse 14 one more time

Peter can end his letter *"Peace to all of you who are in Christ"* because, even in the middle of suffering and trials, we can be perfectly at peace with our Creator because of Jesus' death and resurrection.

31 – BAD TIMES, GOOD TIMES

Read verses 8–11 and use them to guide your prayers today.

v8: Ask God to guide you in life. Talk about specific decisions and situations that are on your mind.

v9: Pray for rescue from stuff that's getting you down and pray that you'll "hide yourself" in God.

v10: Pray that God's will is done. Ask Him to use you to serve Him.

v11–12: Praise God for His perfect righteousness and unfailing love.

33 – THE TRUTH ABOUT GOD

Work out how to answer friends who say God is...

remote

imaginary

uncaring

irrelevant

powerless

nice to everyone

It's good to talk about our own experience of God but it's more important we speak about Jesus' life, death and resurrection.

▶ *How does this help you answer the above views a little better?*

MARK
The end

34 – BIRTH PAINS

Being a Christian shouldn't be easy. We must be prepared to suffer for our faith in Jesus. In some countries (such as Turkey, Sudan, Egypt), Christians are attacked or arrested for following Jesus. That may not happen to us, but we should be ready to tell anyone about Jesus, whoever they are and whatever the consequences. The brilliant thing is that God will help us do it and give us the words to say.

35 – SCARY STUFF

Check out Matthew's version of events in **Matthew 24 v 15–28.**

Jesus is mixing details that are only about the fall of Jerusalem (v15–16, 20) with details about the end of the world (v21).

▶ *What do His followers need to be particularly careful about? (v23–26)*
▶ *What will these fakes be able to do? (v24)*

If we saw someone who could do these things, we'd be impressed! And we'd probably listen to what they had to say — after all, surely someone who can do these amazing feats must be from God?! But Jesus says: "No!" Don't be influenced by someone just because they can do miracles and impressive stuff.

▶ *Flick your eyes down to v35. What counts much more than miracles?*

Don't be impressed by powerful teachers, witty speakers or impressive leaders. Be impressed by those who point you to Jesus' eternal words. We don't need to worry that we might miss Jesus' return. It will be totally obvious to absolutely everyone (v27).

36 – UNMISSABLE

Jesus' teaching on the endtimes is not so much about what we'll find useful when it happens, but how we need to act now.

▶ *So, have you prepared to meet Jesus?*

Now re-read that question.
▶ *Are you really ready?*
▶ *What must you sort out with God now?*
▶ *And how will you now pray for yourself and others you know?*

37 –THE PLOT THICKENS

"Any gospel not centred on Jesus is not good news."
▶ *Can you explain that from today's Bible bit?*
▶ *Why's it vital we keep Jesus' death central in...*
   a) our own walk with God?
   b) our meetings together?
   c) talking about our faith with others?

38 – MEAL DEAL

Read Exodus 12 v 1–14
The lamb was killed instead of the firstborn son in each Israelite family. The blood of the lamb was protection. If there was lamb's blood on the door frame, the Lord would pass over that house. The eldest son could say: *"That lamb died in my place"*.

The lamb's death is a picture of what Jesus would do 1500 years later. He would die on the cross to take the punishment we deserve for our sins against God. Christians can look to Jesus and say: *"He died in my place"*.

If you're a Christian, thank God for sending Jesus to die in your place. Praise Him that on the day of judgment, He will pass over you and not punish you, because of Jesus' death.

39 – THE BREAD OF LIFE
Read verses 22–25 again
"Take it": Jesus' death demands a personal response from us.
"My blood ... is poured out for many": Think what Jesus' death would achieve.

🔵 *Which verses in v1–26 show the sinful human plot going on?*
🔵 *Which show Jesus' control of these final events?*

Because Jesus died, we're free from the penalty of sin — eternal punishment from God. He died for our crime against God. We can be forgiven because He stepped in to pay for our sin.

40 – STAND AND DELIVER
Read Zechariah 13 v 7–9
🔵 *Who is Zechariah pointing to? (v7)*
🔵 *What great comfort can God's people take from v9?*

Christians won't have an easy time. Jesus' disciples saw Him arrested and ran away. Christians around the world continue to suffer in many different ways for following

Jesus. But tough times and persecution help us to become more godly, just as silver is refined by being put through fire (v9). Christians are God's people, and one day He'll gather them to Himself for ever.

41 – GARDEN OF GRIEF
Read verse 36 again
Whenever you read in the Bible about Jesus praying, take note. If you want to improve your prayer times, copy Jesus.

"Abba, Father": Jesus called God "Daddy". Christians are God's children and so can call God "Father" too.
"Everything is possible for you": Praise God for what He's like. Hold on to God's greatness.
"Take this cup from me": Ask God to do what you are unable to do.
"Yet not what I will, but what you will": Recognise that God's will — the way He chooses to answer our prayers — is best. And be obedient.

🔵 *How can this pattern help your praying?*

42 – ARRESTED DEVELOPMENT
Read 1 Peter 2 v 18–25
🔵 *How does Peter tell us to respond to being badly treated? (v18–20)*
🔵 *Why have Christians been "called" to this? (v21)*
🔵 *What is the example Jesus set? (v22–24)*

2 CHRONICLES

43 – IT'S A KING THING

Need a reminder of what's happened in 2 Chronicles so far? Here are the highlights (and lowlights!):

2 Chronicles 1 v 7–12: Sol's wisdom
2 v 1–2: Temple time!
5 v 2–14: Completion celebration
7 v 11–22: God speaks to Solomon
Chapter 10: God's people split
13 v 1–12: Abijah trusting God
14 v 2–6: Asa – obedient and at peace
16 v 11–14: Asa – turning against God

44 – TRUTH OR DARE

For much more on evil Ahab and his run-in with Elijah, check out **1 Kings 16 v 29 – 21 v 29**.

45 – TURN BACK TIME

Read 2 Chronicles 20 v 12

There's no excuse for a Christian to say a situation is hopeless. Even in the worst times, we can say: "Lord, our eyes are on you". God is always with us. We can always look to Him.

▶ *Are you learning the strength of weakness?*
▶ *What should it drive us to do?*
▶ *So, does it?*

47 – WICKED QUEEN OF THE NORTH

Ahaziah's demise gets fuller coverage in **2 Kings 9 v 14–29**. Read it.

▶ *Who was Jehu son of? (v14)*
▶ *What did Jehu think of Joram's reign in Israel? (v22)*

▶ *What did Jehu think of Joram's reign as king of Israel? (v22)*
▶ *What did he do? (v24)*
▶ *Why did this happen to evil King Ahab's son in this particular way? (v25–26)*
▶ *What happened to Judah's king, Ahaziah? (v27–28)*
▶ *How do we see God in control in this gory story?*

48 – KID FOR KING

Read verses 16–17 again
And then Luke 14 v 25–33

▶ *If you're considering becoming a Christian… what's Jesus telling you to do first? (v28–30)*
▶ *If you're already a Christian… what's Jesus telling you following Him will be like? (v27)*

Jesus isn't saying hate your relatives. He's saying you can't follow Him halfheartedly. Either He's your number one, and you're willing to suffer for Him, or you're not. Either you're a 100% follower, or you're no follower at all.

Following Jesus is like running a marathon; it's the finishing that counts, not the starting. Before you start, you must decide to keep going to the finish even when it hurts. Same with following Christ! Still, it's better to be on Jesus' side than opposing Him, just as it's better for a king to be at peace with a stronger king instead of getting slaughtered by him (v31–32).

49 – FROM GOOD TO BAD

Read verses 2 and 17

▶ *When was life sweet with Joash as king?*

▶ *When did it turn sour?*

We're more heavily influenced by the people around us than we think. Christians need other believers to help and encourage and challenge them. To keep them going for God. Finding a more mature Christian to learn from is important. But if we listen to people who don't love God, we'll be pulled away from Him even if we don't see it at the time.

▶ *Who can you meet up with more, who will be a good, godly influence?*

▶ *Who do you need to stop hanging out with?*

50 – ANOTHER FINE MESS

Read verses 7–9 again

This is a message often repeated in Chronicles — If you live for God you'll be blessed; if you abandon God He'll abandon you. God gives us chances to turn back to Him. Don't pass up the opportunity.

▶ *What's the message when we think we'll lose out by living God's way? (v9)*

Read Mark 10 v 28–30

51 – LOUD AND PROUD

Read Isaiah 6 v 1–7

▶ *King Uzziah ruled Judah for 52 years. But who's the real king? (v1)*

▶ *How did the seraphs ("burning ones") show their respect for God? (v2)*

▶ *What big truth about God did they shout? (v3)*

▶ *How did Isaiah respond to the sight of perfect, holy God on His throne? (v5)*

▶ *What did he confess? (v5)*

▶ *So what did God do for Isaiah? (v6–7)*

52 – GOOD KING, BAD KING

Read what God thought about Ahaz in Isaiah 7 v 1–17

▶ *What was God's message to Ahaz? (v4, v9)*

God told Ahaz to forget about politics and trust God to rescue His people. Ahaz refused, so God spoke again.

▶ *What did God want Ahaz to do? (v11)*

▶ *But what did He do? (v12)*

God's angry response (v13–17) sounds weird but it was a picture message. The virgin (God's people) would give birth to a son (a faithful remnant who trusted God) and God would be with them. But Ahaz (and anyone who refused God's help) would face God's punishment. Verse 14 points us forward to Jesus (Immanuel) who'd be born as a human baby — He would be God living with His people. Ahaz refused God's help so Judah would face the consequences. No one and no part of the land would escape God's judgment.

53 – HEROIC HEZEKIAH

Here's what Michael Wilcock said about the start of Hezekiah's reign:

"The world expects everyone to react to a crisis in terms of that crisis. And the church, if it is sufficiently infected with worldliness, will readily oblige. When we have a financial crisis, the first thing we think about is money ... If Hezekiah had responded to a military threat in a military way, the Assyrians would have understood that. Army would have been matched against army, with dire consequences for Judah. But instead Hezekiah first looked to God. Were he and his people right with God? Was God's temple open, clean, glorious with offerings and praise? The result was that when the invaders did reach Jerusalem, the presence of God filled it and it was impregnable."
(From The Message of Chronicles, published by IVP.)

54 – GREAT INVITATION

**Read John 1 v 29–31
and then 1 Corinthians 5 v 7
and finally 1 Peter 1 v 17–21**

▶ *How does the Passover point us to Jesus Christ?*

55 – SUPPORTING GOD'S WORK

Read Deuteronomy 14 v 22–29

▶ *What must the Israelites do with a tenth of their good stuff? (v23)*

▶ *Why? (end of v23)*

▶ *Who else should they look after? (v28–29)*

There are loads of laws in Deuteronomy chapters 12–26 — most of them specifically for God's people in Old Testament times. When Jesus came, He took the place of these laws. But they still have great principles we can follow. Giving a *"tithe"* (tenth) of your money and possessions to God's work (church, missionaries, Christian charities) is a good principle many Christians follow. Some give loads more than that. We should also financially support Christian workers who aren't so well-off and look after those who have less than us.

56 – TERRIFYING ENEMY

Read about Hezekiah's illness and what he wrote after God cured him in
Isaiah 38 v 1–22.

▶ *What do the four images in v12–14 say about how Hez felt?*

▶ *But what brought an amazing turnaround? (v15–16)*

▶ *How did he view his suffering? (v17)*

God rescued Hezekiah from death. Guess what, He does the same for us! On the cross, Jesus defeated sin and death for ever. Everyone who trusts in Him will live for ever with God.

57 – MAN MONSTER

What's more incredible: Manasseh's evil or his repentance? Compare him with Saul/Paul in **Acts 7 v 59 – 8 v 1,
Acts 9 v 1–19,
and 1 Timothy 1 v 13–16.**

It's been said: "If God could save Paul, he can save me". If God can turn around the life of Manasseh, he can do the same for me, no matter what I've done.

▶ Do you believe this?
▶ What effect will it have on your life?

58 – THE LOST BOOK
Read verses 19–21 and 31 again
Maybe Josiah was first reading part of Deuteronomy chapter 28, about the curses for not obeying God's covenant.

▶ What makes Josiah's attitude to God's word a good one?
▶ Will you ask God to sort out your attitude too?

59 – THE LAST GREAT KING?
Read verse 25 and then Jeremiah 22 v 11–30
▶ What was God's message to these kings?
▶ And the reason for it?
▶ What truths are we reminded of?

60 – JUDAH IN RUINS
Read verses 20–23 again
Despite this shattering judgment, the story of God and His people would continue. At the end of 2 Chronicles, we're left waiting for a leader who can really sort out God's people. We're waiting for God to send His Son to rule as King on earth. Thank God for all you've learned from 2 Chronicles. And praise Him for Jesus, the perfect King.

61 – SHOUT OUT TO GOD
Stop and briefly analyse your prayer time.
▶ What do you normally talk to God about first?
▶ In what attitude do you talk to Him? Is it a) routine? b) like a robot? c) without thinking? d) rushed? e) something else?

Now read Matthew 6 v 5–13
Jesus says don't pretend when praying (v5–6). And don't babble (v7–8). But recognise who it is you're talking to (v8–10). And only then, start asking.
▶ Need to make some changes to the way you talk to God?

62 – RAISE THE PRAISE
▶ How is God attractive?
▶ What is it about Him that's incredible and irresistible?
▶ What do you want to tell other people about Him?

Read 1 John 4 v 9–10
▶ How can you use these verses to explain God's love to a non-Christian?

MARK

63 – THE END
Read verses 61–62 again and then Daniel 7 v 13–14
▶ What do we learn here about the "Son of Man"?

Use Daniel 7 v 13–14 as you pray, praising Jesus for who He really is.

64 – TRIAL AND ERROR
Read John 21 v 15–19
▷ *What does Jesus ask Simon Peter?*
▷ *Why do you think He asks him three times?*
▷ *What job does He give Peter? (v17)*
▷ *How will Peter die? (v18–19)*

This was actually wonderful news for Peter. Jesus says Peter would be able to stay loyal to his Lord even when Peter was facing his own death!

65 – BAD CALL
Read Isaiah 53 v 1–12
God crushed His own Son. But not because Jesus deserved it — it was the only way to pay for our disgusting sins and our rebellion against God. Jesus was prepared to go through terrible pain, suffering and loneliness for pathetic sinners like us! Incredible.

It's the most outrageous swap: Jesus gets punished; sinful people get pardoned, forgiven. All of which begs a question: will you rely on yourself or on what Jesus has done for you? Only you know exactly what you need to say to God right now. Make sure you do so.

67 – CRUCIFIED
Read Psalm 22 v 7–18
This is no freaky coincidence. According to Hebrews 2 v 12, we can hear the words of Psalm 22 as Jesus' own. It's mind-boggling that this song, so clearly telling us about Jesus' last hours, was composed hundreds of years before His death.

Now read Psalm 22 v 23–31
▷ *What does Jesus call us to do? (v23–24)*
▷ *What will be the world's response now and in the future? (v30–31)*

This psalm is like reading an interview with the Saviour of the world, even as the rescue takes place! It reveals that through excruciating agony and humiliation, Jesus saw the bigger picture — God being honoured as future generations hear His message of ultimate love. As He died, you were on His mind. Now re-read v23–31, and join in worshipping the God who gave His Son for you.

68 – WHY DID JESUS DIE?
Read verses 33–34 once more
The darkness symbolises God's judgment — Jesus was enduring the withdrawal of God, His loving Father, who'd loved Jesus perfectly since before time began. God turned His back on His Son because Jesus took our sin upon Himself.

Now read Psalm 22 v 1–5
Jesus quoted v1; v3–5 tells of God's trustworthiness. Jesus didn't stop trusting God on the cross. In quoting Psalm 22, He's affirmed His faith in God and that His death was the death of the Christ that had been foretold in the Old Testament.

69 – FINAL BREATH
▷ Read Hebrews 10 v 19–25
Because of everything we've learned about Jesus, our high priest, we can be sure of a welcome from God. Because of

what Jesus has done for us, we can *"draw near to God with a sincere heart"* (v22) — a heart that doesn't cover stuff up. Jesus' sacrifice has wiped us clean from guilt. So, trust in what Jesus has done, and be free from fear when you come to God.

71 – THE BIG FINALE

There is serious doubt whether Mark 16 v 9–20 should be a part of Mark's Gospel. These verses don't appear in the earliest manuscripts so it seems that some people were frustrated by the way this book ended and added their own "appropriate" ending! Mark's Gospel ends with the women terrified and no mention of Jesus actually appearing after His resurrection (you'll find that in Matthew's, Luke's and John's Gospels). But this ending still works brilliantly. We're left with a sense of awe and wonder at what has just happened. And shouldn't that be how Jesus' life, death and resurrection leaves us?

2 PETER

72 – EVERYTHING WE NEED

1 Peter has shown us how the Christian life has a beginning, a middle and an end.
Beginning: You respond to God's gospel message of total forgiveness because of Jesus' death. You're born again; you become alive to God (1 Peter 1 v 18–25).

Middle: You carry on trusting God's gospel message and aim to obey Jesus day by day. Suffering is still a fact of life. 1 Peter 4 v 1–5 sums up this stage.

End: You go to be with Jesus for ever. Suffering ends for ever. Sin can't spoil your friendship with Jesus because you've got a new nature (1 Peter 5 v 10).

74 – REFRESHING YOUR MEMORY

Read verses 16–18 again followed by Matthew 17 v 1–8
When Peter thinks back to this experience, it makes him all the more certain that Jesus will come back again. Here's why: as God's Son, Jesus is the rightful ruler of the whole world. The world doesn't realise that yet, but it will when Jesus comes back in the kind of spectacular glory He had on this mountain. Peter was an eye-witness to the fact Jesus is God's Son, the world's rightful ruler.

75 – RELIGIOUS CONMEN

Read verse 4 again. It's probably referring to the strange events of **Genesis 6 v 1–4**. It could also be talking about Satan and his followers being thrown out of heaven (**Luke 10 v 18; Revelation 12 v 7–9**). Whatever Peter's referring to, his point is this: no one is exempt from God's judgment, not even angels. And though God may not punish sin immediately, He WILL punish sin. The great news is that Jesus' death offers us a way to be rescued from God's judgment.

76 – WASHED PIGS

The conmen might have said something like: *"Peter's insurance policy is alright for beginners, but you must move on. Don't worry about this self-control thing; what you do with your body doesn't matter. Get drunk; have sex with who you like. It's the spiritual part of you that counts. You want to be really spiritual? Then you need the special knowledge we've got."* But Peter tells his readers they already have the knowledge they need. See how often the word "knowledge" appears in 1 v 1–11.

78 –WAIT, WATCH

Read verse 13 again;
then look at Revelation 21 v 1–7

▶ *Why is heaven worth waiting for?*

▶ *How does this description of heaven differ from what we currently experience?*

▶ *Why does it encourage us to live God's way?*

79 – READY, STEADY, GROW

Read through all of 2 Peter in one go.

▶ *What does Peter say about knowledge?*

▶ *What is the way to be a stable and effective Christian, and not a wobbly and useless one?*

PROVERBS

80 – HARD HITTING WORDS

Look at verses 11–15

▶ *Which of these proverbs about words applies to you most?*

▶ *What do you think God is saying to you?*

▶ *What action will you take?*

81 – FOOL'S GOLD

Read verses 4–5 once more

Do these verses contradict each other? Here's what Graham Goldsworthy says: *"The apparent contradiction involved is resolved when we realise that proverbs are usually based on observations of specific events. Thus, one situation is best handled by refusing to play the fool's game with him, while another demands some [response] to his folly. Life is full of both kinds of situations, and these two sayings remind us that there is no clear-cut response. One must assess each situation carefully and decide whether to engage the fool or disengage from his company."* (Taken from "The Tree of Life", available from www.thegoodbook.co.uk)

82 – FRIENDLY ADVICE

Read verse 1 again,
and then James 4 v 13–17

▶ *Why is it wrong to boast about the future?*

Our plans need to fit in with God's plans for us. We must seek His will for our lives. Think about your major plans for the next month, year and 5 years. How do they reflect your attitude to God and your priorities in life?

84 – MIXED BAG

Read verse 13
followed by 1 John 1 v 5–10

Spend time confessing recent sins to God, who forgives everyone who trusts in His Son. Then turn v9 into your own prayer of praise.

85 – SOL'S SMART SAYINGS

One of Solomon's themes in Proverbs is "How a good ruler should behave". See 16 v 10–12; 17 v 7; 20 v 8, 26 and 28. And 29 v 2, 4, 12, 14.

▶ What picture of a good ruler do they give?

▶ How does King Jesus fully show all these good qualities?

86 – MYSTERY MAN'S WISE WORDS

Read verses 5–6 again, followed by Revelation 22 v 18–19 and Psalm 18 v 30–36

88 – SEX, BOOZE AND JUSTICE

Check out these Bible verses about alcohol:
Psalm 104 v 14–15
1 Timothy 5 v 23
Proverbs 20 v 1
Proverbs 23 v 31–35
Ephesians 5 v 18

89 – IT'S A WONDERFUL WIFE

Are you single and unhappy? (Or married and unhappy?) If chapter 31 has struck a raw nerve for you, ask God to give you another dose of patience, trust and wisdom for the future.

The Bible tells us that the church (all Christians) are the "bride of Christ".

▶ So how does chapter 31 apply to all Christians and how we should live?

90 – PRAISE PARTY

Read verses 5 and 13, and then Exodus 3 v 13–15

His name, the Lord, revealed who He is — the great, almighty, living God.

Read verses 7–10 again

It's a strange idea. How can animals praise God? Well, surely by being what they are: as creatures under God's authority carrying out the function He's given them to do.

Read Genesis 1 v 26–28

What's the role of humans, then? Well, we're to praise God by living in His world as He intended us to: recognising His right to run our lives, and our responsibility to rule and use wisely everything God has given us. That way our lives praise God.

91 – SONGS AND SWORDS

Read verse 6; then Hebrews 4 v 12, and Ephesians 6 v 17

▶ Does this change your attitude to God's word?

▶ Who do you need to pray for, who has heard the gospel but not responded to God?

92 – THE BIG FINISH

Read Ephesians 1 v 3–23

▶ Why should we praise God? (v3–14 is not short of ideas)

▶ How should we pray for others? (v15–23 gives help)

▶ Why not use this chapter as a basis for your time with God?

RSVP

engage wants to hear from YOU!

▶ Share experiences of God at work in your life
▶ Any questions you have about the Bible or the Christian life?
▶ How can we make *engage* better?

Email us — martin@thegoodbook.co.uk

Or send us snail mail to: engage, Unit B1, Blenheim House, 1 Blenheim Road, Epsom, Surrey, KT19 9AP, UK

engage covers the whole Bible in 20 issues. Missing any?

Order **engage** now!

Make sure you order any issues of **engage** you've not read yet. Or even better, grab a one-year subscription to make sure **engage** lands in your hands four times a year!

Call us to order in the UK on 0333 123 0880
International: +44 (0) 20 8942 0880

or visit your friendly neighbourhood website:
UK: www.thegoodbook.co.uk
N America: www.thegoodbook.com
Australia: www.thegoodbook.com.au
New Zealand: www.thegoodbook.co.nz

Growing
with God

Faithful, contemporary Bible reading resources for every age and stage.

Beginning with God
For pre-schoolers

Table Talk & XTB
Table Talk for 4-11s and their parents, *XTB* for 7-11s

Discover
For 11-13s

Engage
For 14-18s

Explore
For adults

All Good Book Company Bible reading resources...

- ❯ have a strong focus on practical application
- ❯ encourage people to read the Bible for themselves
- ❯ explain Bible passages in context
- ❯ cover Bible books in the Old and New Testament

FREE *Explore* App for iOS and Android.

Download today from the App Store or Android Market

UK: www.thegoodbook.co.uk
N America: www.thegoodbook.com
Australia: www.thegoodbook.com.au
New Zealand: www.thegoodbook.co.nz

thegoodbook
COMPANY